ABOUT THE AUTHOR

Humble the Poet (a.k.a. Kanwer Singh) is a Canadian-born artist, rapper, spoken-word poet, international best-selling author, and former elementary school teacher. He is the author of *The Globe and Mail* best-seller *Unlearn*, *Things No One Else Can Teach Us*, and *How to Be Love(d)*. With his tattoos, beard, head wrap, and silly smile, Humble commands attention. He stimulates audiences with ideas that challenge conventional wisdom and go against the grain, with dynamic live sets that shake conventions and minds at the same time. He has performed at concerts and festivals, including Lollapalooza, and has been featured in major media including *The New York Times*, *BuzzFeed*, *Vogue*, *Rolling Stone*, and *Huffington Post*.

Visit him at **humblethepoet.com** and **@humblethepoet.**

Also by Humble the Poet

*How to Be Love(d): Simple Truths for Going Easier on Yourself, Embracing Imperfection & Loving Your Way to a Better Life**

Things No One Else Can Teach Us

Unlearn: 101 Simple Truths for a Better Life

*Available from Hay House

Please visit:

Hay House India: www.hayhouse.co.in
Hay House USA: www.hayhouse.com®
Hay House Australia: www.hayhouse.com.au
Hay House UK: www.hayhouse.co.uk

UN ANXIOUS

50 SIMPLE TRUTHS TO HELP OVERTHINKERS FEEL LESS STRESS AND MORE CALM

HAY HOUSE

HAY HOUSE INDIA
New Delhi • London • Sydney
Carlsbad, California • New York City

Hay House Publishers (India) Pvt Ltd
Muskaan Complex, Plot No. 3, B-2, Vasant Kunj, New Delhi – 110070, India

Hay House LLC, P.O. Box 5100, Carlsbad, CA 92018-5100, USA
Hay House UK Ltd, 1st Floor, Crawford Corner, 91-93 Baker Street, London W1U 6QQ, UK
Hay House Australia Publishing Pty Ltd, 18/36 Ralph St., Alexandria NSW 2015, Australia

Email: contact@hayhouse.co.in
Website: www.hayhouse.co.in

Cover design: Julie Davison
Interior design: Karim J. Garcia

First published by Hay House India, 2025
10 9 8 7 6 5 4 3 2 1

ISBN 978-93-6611-142-1

Printed at Repro India Limited

FSC
www.fsc.org
MIX
Paper from responsible sources
FSC® C047271

Hay House is committed to a sustainable future for our business, our readers and our planet. This book is made from Forest Stewardship Council® certified paper.

Anxiety is not a weakness.
It's a sign that you're paying attention.

— WENDY WALSH, PH.D.

CONTENTS

SCAN THIS OR FOREVER WONDER WHAT YOU MISSED

Seriously, it's just sitting there. Mysterious.
Waiting. Bonus chapters are calling your name.

0.

INTRODUCTION

The Cure for Anxiety

Unclench your jaw.

Gently take your tongue off the roof of your mouth and let it rest.

Are you holding your breath? Let go.

Breathe in, saying "*in*" in your mind.

As you exhale, say "*drop*" in your mind, and let your shoulders fall.

I hate that you had to pick up this book. Every time I mention I'm working on a book about anxiety, people lean in—eager for an early copy or to declare themselves the perfect guinea pig.

I hate that life has become so overwhelming, so stressful, that you picked up this book hoping for a few magical words to make it all go away.

I hate that now I see everything through a lens of anxiety. I see it in the people who hurt me, and in the friends slowly killing themselves to chase an invisible prize called success.

We wouldn't need a book like this if everyone could get a big bear hug from someone they feel safe with and have them whisper, "It's okay, you're not broken, you're not alone, you don't have to be scared anymore."

But we don't all have that, and even if we do, we're so afraid of bothering them and feeling rejection that we isolate ourselves further, not wanting to be a burden.

That's why this book is here.*

* And when you need it, you can always open it, stick your face in and give yourself a book hug—it's not a bear hug, but it'll do.

Before you dive into this book, wrap it up as a gift, or take a picture of it next to your dog, a latte, or those fancy candles you never actually light; I want you to know something:

There's nothing wrong with you.

You don't need to be fixed. The anxious feelings you have aren't your fault, and the sometimes damaging things you do to avoid, medicate, or suppress those feelings aren't a sign that you're a piece of shit. They're signs you're a beautifully normal human being trying their best in a world that promises us that we can feel better, but then beats the shit out of us so we feel worse.

You're not the only person who feels like they're drowning while everyone else has it figured out.

No one has figured it out.

Everyone's feeling anxious. And even as we start to deal with that anxiety, we discover more layers, some generational, some ancient, and some so deep they feel like tattoos on our souls.

I'm not here to promise I can get rid of all your anxious feelings. I literally wrote the book on anxiety and still feel anxious. The difference now is I don't hate, avoid, or hit the snooze button on those feelings as much anymore. I respect and listen to them, and sometimes* I'm even thankful they're there.

What I *can* promise is that I know what it feels like to cling to anything and everything that might make these shitty feelings go away, and the last thing I'd ever do is disrespect you by telling you some bullshit and pretending to have a quick fix or magic pill.

Instead, I invite you on a journey to see anxiety through a new lens. Along the way you will find new ways to understand and embrace overwhelming feelings, leading to less stress and more calm.

I hate that you needed to pick up this book, but you did, and here we are, and I promise that if you read these words with an open mind and heart, you'll never view anxiety as the enemy again.

* Just sometimes.

Let's get started:

If you turn to page 137, on the bottom of the page, a little off-center to the left, you'll find a secret compartment. In that compartment, you'll find two magic pills. Take those pills with three whole glasses of water, and you will be cured of anxiety forever. Wait, did you really do it?

Now that I've lost all your trust, let's continue.

There's no cure for anxiety. Not because it's incurable like our addiction to cat videos, but because **anxiety isn't something that needs curing.**

It's not a contagious disease you caught in the air or from kissing someone who forgot to brush their teeth. Anxiety isn't cooties, dandruff, or herpes. It's not something we have to rid ourselves of; it's something we have to manage—like hunger. And like hunger, it's going to come back; it's just part of having a brain and feelings.

Simply put: Anxiety is our brain's way of signaling us to pay attention.

Not-so-simply put: Anxiety is the uncomfortable feeling we get when our **amygdala**—the "survival brain"—*thinks* there's a threat. When this happens, our survival brain takes control away from our **prefrontal cortex**—the "logical brain"—and sets off anxiety. These feelings arise because our bodies flood us with chemicals like adrenaline and cortisol to prepare us for a threat.

This can happen when something or someone reminds our survival brain of:

- Times we felt unsafe or threatened.
- Moments when we lost control.
- Experiences that left a painful mark.
- The fear of being rejected or left out.
- Worries about failing or letting others down.

Those reminders are what we call **triggers**. When these triggers pop up, our survival brain reacts quickly, often before we notice. That's why we might feel a surge of anxiety without knowing the reason.

Think of it like this: the logical brain is the tortoise, and the survival brain is the hare. When we're triggered, the hare takes off! Our job is to make sure the slow-and-steady tortoise still wins the race.*

* And no, we're not allowed to shoot the hare.

Much like shivering when we're cold, sweating when we're hot, and drooling when we sleep,* anxiety is a reaction and a much-needed form of protection that's been helping us survive since we were eating wooly mammoth burgers. As unpleasant as shivering, sweating, or drooling are, we understand that they're normal and natural ways for our body to react to things happening in and around us, just like yawning, hiccuping, laughing, crying, and burping.

Most of the time, there isn't a real threat—just an imagined one setting off a false alarm—leaving us feeling uneasy and on edge without knowing why.

This happens because our survival brain isn't just on the lookout for real threats; it's constantly predicting them based on past experiences. Instead of asking, "What's actually happening right now?" our brain asks, "What does this remind me of from the past?" This often leads to overreacting, sensing danger where there isn't any, and blowing things out of proportion.

Since our anxiety is triggered way more frequently than it's needed, we often try to push away anxious feelings instead of checking if there's really a problem. While coping mechanisms can make us feel better for a while, they're just a snooze button and lead to more stress later on. This is why we sometimes feel anxious and have no idea why—it's because an alarm we snoozed earlier is blaring again.

So once again, I can't cure your anxiety, because it doesn't need to be cured. What I can do is cure the despair you feel around being overwhelmed with these anxious feelings.

Despair is the stress we feel when we think we've run out of options. It's the feeling of hopelessness when we don't know what else we can do.

Well, my handsome friend, I'm about to rock your world with a gang of tips to help you soothe your anxiety more quickly and experience it less often.

The way we're going to do that is by looking at four parts of our life:**

- **Our Environments:** The places we frequent and the company we keep. Even those imaginary friends count.

---

* I've said too much.

** You'll see those labels at the beginning of each chapter.

- **Our Habits:** Get ready to admit you bring your phone to the toilet. It's a judgment-free zone.
- **Our Thoughts:** Our mindsets and beliefs. All those weird thoughts you have in the shower or why you think that one text is the end of the world.
- **Our Reactions:** How we deal with stress and anxiety automatically. Because screaming into a pillow or running off to join the circus isn't always the answer.

So, instead of seeing this book as a magic pill,* think of it like a sweater. You can wear it to shiver less, take it off to sweat less, or ball it up and stuff it in your mouth to drool less.

We can't think our way out of anxiety; we have to act our way through it. Those actions come from our behaviors, and those behaviors are strengthened by our practices.

Absorbing the simple truths in this book will help your logical brain understand anxiety, but it's the practice and consistency that will teach your survival brain to chill out. Managing emotions is a skill, and like any skill, it takes time and effort to improve.**

You're not going to finish this book and suddenly live anxiety-free. Instead, you'll walk away with a big, sexy tool belt full of options for when anxious feelings start creeping in. That tool belt won't make life lighter, but it'll make you stronger and more ready to handle a world that only gets heavier.

You're a fucking champ, and this book will guide you through understanding and managing one of the most misunderstood emotions: anxiety.

Remember, it's not always about what we can do to feel better, but how we can stop fueling our own suffering.

Also, now that your grubby fingerprints are all over page 137, this book is officially "used," and no, there are no refunds.

* Apparently hiding magic pills in books that ship worldwide is somehow a crime.

** You need to keep practicing these skills, and I'll keep revisiting them throughout the book so they really sink in. That way, they'll stick with you when you need them most.

WE CAN'T THINK OUR WAY OUT OF ANXIETY; WE HAVE TO ACT OUR WAY THROUGH IT.

HUMBLE THE POET

PART 1:

UNDERSTANDING ANXIETY

1.

ENVIRONMENTS

WE'RE WIRED TO WORRY

When I was 13, I met my great-grandmother for the first time and handed her the first cold bottle of Coca-Cola she ever had in her 100+ years. She had lived her whole life in a village around Rajasthan where my father was born. Both of my parents grew up in villages without electricity, and my uncle told me he hadn't seen a light bulb until he was 13 himself. Years later, I took my parents to the villages of the Maasai Mara in Kenya, and my mother immediately was hit with joyful nostalgia, as it all reminded her of her childhood in Punjab.

Though by now they've spent most of their lives in Canada, my parents grew up in small villages, and it's still evident in the speed that they live their life. If we all trace lineages back far enough, we'll realize we're all originally from small communities like a village.

Imagine firelit gatherings from a thousand years ago, where faces flicker in the warm glow. Everyone knows each other, dangers are shared, and support is always there. Now, fast-forward to a modern city—honking horns, flashing screens, and streets full of strangers. We crave connection but feel completely alone. This is the paradox of modern life.

Our brains, designed for survival in tight-knit communities, now struggle to keep up. Back then, threats were clear: a hungry predator, a rival tribe. Today's anxieties are more elusive: a never-ending inbox, the pressure to constantly "grind," the fear of missing out (FOMO).

Sure, modern life means we no longer have to poop outside, marry our cousins, or worry about being sacrificial virgins, but even with all of humanity's leaps into the future, **our brains are still ancient, and they just can't keep up with these new modern triggers.**

These modern triggers are known as **novel stressors**—new challenges that our prehistoric brains weren't built to handle. Things like traffic jams, social media drama, and the constant push to achieve fall into this category. I've actually quit driving because I had too many anxiety attacks stuck in traffic. I'd rather navigate the obstacle course of New York sidewalks or play "what's that smell" on the subway any day over being behind the wheel.

It's not that life was easy for our hunter-gatherer ancestors. Sure, they didn't face traffic jams, but they also lived with the constant threat of starvation, disease, and exposure to dangerous animals.* The key difference? They faced these challenges together.

Back then and now, it's important to remember that **anxiety isn't a personal issue. It's something we all experience and need to tackle together.**

Social connection is the missing piece. To borrow a word from political scientist Robert Putnam, our **social capital**—meaning the web of connections that binds us—is shrinking. Beyond home and work, we need a third place to connect with others. Losing these spaces, like parks and community centers, makes us feel more isolated. While it's good that people aren't going to bars and drinking as much, it would be better if they found other places to gather,** because now it seems like most of our socializing happens on the phone. These days, I mostly talk to my close friends through chat groups on my phone. I don't see their faces or hear their voices, and that feels lonely.

Modern life can often make us feel ashamed, isolated, and anxious. Instead of reaching for success, we're often just trying not to fail. This ongoing pressure wears down our self-worth and leaves us feeling uneasy.

Take social media, for example. We're constantly seeing 25-year-olds with perfect bodies and luxurious lives, making us feel like we're not measuring up to impossible standards.

* And humans.

** . . . Or lived that mocktail life.

For most millennials and zoomers, owning a home feels out of reach because of high student debt and living expenses. The struggle to be financially secure in a challenging economy only adds to our anxiety.*

When we feel unworthy of basic needs like safety, love, and self-expression, we often blame ourselves and turn to distractions or medications to cope. This makes us easy prey in a system that profits from keeping us anxious, competitive, and always spending.

I'm not suggesting we go back to living in small villages and pooping outside again, but knowing that our brains are still wired for a different time can help us make better choices today.

Modern life isn't all bad. We can use technology to make our lives better without losing our connections with people. Research by Donald Appleyard shows that well-designed neighborhoods with less traffic help build a sense of community. Imagine parks full of laughter, busy libraries, and community centers where people support each other.

Instead of trying to get rid of or ignore our anxiety, we need to change how our brain handles stress. Focusing on bringing back third places and community helps us connect with others and build resilience. By creating and using these spaces, we can support each other and reduce anxiety. **Facing challenges together in supportive environments makes us stronger and helps us feel less alone.** Stepping out of our comfort zones strengthens the part of our brain that controls motivation and emotions.

Don't blame yourself for struggling. The pressure you feel is real, and it's not your fault. Society often values convenience over resilience, making us always busy. This chapter isn't about hating modern conveniences; it's about finding ways to stay connected and healthy.

The good news? You're not alone. Let's face the challenges of modern life together and create a future where connection and community are key to a happy life.

---

* I still don't understand how my taxi driver dad and Kellogg's factory worker mom were able to afford and pay off a mortgage for a house in the Toronto city limits.

All my grandparents and great-grandparents have since passed. The villages my parents grew up in all have Wi-Fi now, and as the family grew, the sense of community shrunk. The plots of land that my ancestors owned are being sold as we have no immediate family left in India to watch them. What we owned for hundreds of years will sell for enough to barely get a one-bedroom condo in the sky. Although it's the death of those communities, it's an opportunity for me to take ownership to create my own. Not simply through the groups in my phone, but through the groups I build in person—whether that's my jiujitsu gang, the dog park friends, the friends I've made in my building,* or my childhood friends who I still take trips with.

* Whose names I always forget.

DON'T BLAME YOURSELF FOR STRUGGLING. THE PRESSURE YOU FEEL IS REAL, AND IT'S NOT YOUR FAULT.

THOUGHTS

2. ANXIETY OVERESTIMATES THE THREAT & UNDERESTIMATES OUR ABILITY TO DEAL WITH IT

Have you ever gotten the dreaded "Can we talk?" text? Suddenly, your mind turns into a Formula 1 race car, zooming through all the possible disasters: "Did I forget their birthday? Did they figure out you're still using their Netflix password? Did I say something dumb three weeks ago at brunch?" None of this has happened yet, but our survival brain is already panicking for the worst-case scenario.

We have a cognitive bias called **catastrophizing**; it's the tendency to jump to the worst-case scenario. When we're anxious, our minds race ahead, filling in the blanks with the worst things possible. We see this a lot in social situations, where anxiety quietly saddles up beside us and whispers, "What if nobody here likes you?"

We're always told, "Hope for the best; prepare for the worst," but most of the time, we're only hoping for the best and really prepared for nothing. That's because it makes us anxious to think about the worst.

Look, I'm not here to Bob Marley your anxiety with "every little thing's gonna be alright," because honestly, sometimes things are not alright. But here's the good news: even if everything goes horribly wrong, you're a strong little birdy tough enough to handle it.

So many of us are afraid of rejection and probably have an intense story of having our hearts ripped out of our chests and stomped on, and then piece by piece, kicked into a muddy pond. The emotions we felt with that experience now have us understandably avoiding anything that even resembles another heartbreak. The obvious truths about our past heartbreaks are: we survived them, and remembering our ability to survive them can give us confidence to survive the next.

Anxiety overestimates the danger and underestimates our ability to deal with it. Remember: **our nervous system isn't reacting to things; it's predicting them.** That means our nervous system takes in information, and then compares the thing in front of us to something we've already experienced and decides that the same emotional reaction, however unhelpful, is the best way to address the situation.

This isn't because our survival brains hate us; it's because they give that emotional reaction too much credit for our survival. So, if overthinking, overanalyzing, and freaking out helped us "survive" from an imaginary danger last time, our brain decides to do it again whenever a situation rhymes with that danger.

We're constantly looking at life through the lens of old experiences while we're in a dysregulated state, which means we react on autopilot. That reaction is us catastrophizing.

- *Someone seems unhappy with us; let's jump into pleasing people.*
- *A conflict's brewing? Better hide under a pile of laundry.*
- *Hear a weird noise in the basement? Obviously, it's a monster giving a serial killer a piggyback ride. Might as well pack up and move to New Zealand.*

Sometimes this is out of our control; no one knows when a trigger will happen, and we're all caught off guard. But what about the times we know something may happen?

When we make new choices to regulate our nervous system and retrain our survival brain, we won't rely on old, outdated ways to cope, and our brain will learn more options for the next "threat." Having more options means less despair.

Our mind will always exaggerate threats, and that will leave us feeling overwhelmed and helpless. Our survival brain is a drama queen, constantly amplifying threats we face, calling small hiccups catastrophes, and hurting our confidence to handle them. Anxiety is fear rehearsing failure—by repeatedly imagining the worst, we limit our confidence and ability to act.

Feeling your anxiety won't kill you, but avoiding it just might.

Fear is a mile-wide ocean, and it's overwhelming to look at. But once you step in, you realize it's only an inch deep. The truth is, bad things will happen; there will be loss, challenges, and death, but none of that will be the end of you. You're more resilient than you think.

I'm not saying there aren't real risks;* but most of the bad things that happen aren't situations we can predict and prepare for. It's important to stay aware of potential dangers, but instead of blindly trusting our survival brains take on them, we should slow down, take a breath,** and let our logical brain assess how likely and severe those dangers really are.

For instance, being alone at a party can be uncomfortable, and it's not impossible that someone points you out to the whole room and starts teasing you, but that's more likely on some goofy TV show than in real life. If you witness someone being singled out at a party and made fun of, you wouldn't join in. We know most people are decent, and most social interactions are forgiving and positive.

While anxiety thrives on magnifying threats, it also minimizes our capabilities. It whispers in our ears, "You're not strong enough; you're not capable; you'll never overcome this."

Underestimating our own strength keeps us trapped in a cycle of fear and inaction. It's a self-fulfilling prophecy: if we believe we're incapable of handling challenges, we're less likely to even try. This is our brain's weird way of protecting us by making us do nothing, which it thinks will keep us safe.

The truth is we're far more resilient and capable than our anxious feelings lead us to believe. Our personal history is filled with inspiring stories of us facing fears head-on and making it out the other end in one piece.

New experiences are supposed to create anxious feelings, because we don't know where we are and have no idea what to do. But as time goes on, we

* Like eating sushi at a gas station.

** Or ten.

gain clarity, things feel like they slow down, and we have a better grasp of things. We can't skip steps in this progress toward calm and clarity; we can only remind ourselves this is the process.

I spent years flirting with the idea of doing jiujitsu. I'm a huge fan of mixed martial arts, and after a few years of boxing, I finally decided to take the plunge. Coincidentally, the highest-rated school in the city was only a few blocks away, but I still procrastinated for months. I was scared—scared of getting hurt, beat up, bullied, and not making progress. Being in a new city and starting jiujitsu in my 40s felt like an anxious cherry on top of an already anxious sundae.

When I finally went for my intro session, everyone was so kind. The instructors were welcoming, and about a month in, the head instructor pulled me aside and said, "You look very interesting. What do you do for a living?" When I told him I'm a writer, he excitedly said, "I knew it," and immediately bought my books on his phone.

This felt less like having a *Karate Kid* sensei and more like a bunch of friends training together. Over the next couple of months, I did get beat up a lot and had to take time off for injuries, but that's part of the deal with martial arts.

Instead of running into overly aggressive bullies, I met a lot of younger guys who, despite being twice my size and more skilled, were surprisingly shy when asking if I wanted to hang out after class—right after choking me out, of course.

A year in, I still suck, but my emotional regulation has improved a lot. My survival brain finally caught up to my logical brain, realizing that no one here is trying to hurt me. Things feel slower now, and I get overwhelmed much less. I'm familiar with the rough-and-tumble nature of the sport, and my nervous system has graduated past freeze, past fight-or-flight, into a place of safety. Even when I'm overmatched, I find myself more excited to learn what my training partners did to me than feeling anxious or unsafe.

I took my catastrophizing brain for a spin, and it wasn't nearly as terrifying as I thought. Turns out, jiujitsu is less about getting choked out and more about making friends who just happen to choke you out for fun. And it all started with that baby step of showing up for my first class.

Remember, courage isn't the absence of fear; it's choosing to move forward DESPITE it.

Anxious feelings may seem like an unbeatable enemy, but we have the power to challenge how it overestimates risks, recognize our strengths, and face problems head-on. Here are some practical tips to help regain control over anxiety:

- **Challenge catastrophic thoughts:** When anxiety kicks in, question it. Ask yourself, "Is this really going to happen? What are the more realistic outcomes?" Chances are, it's not as bad as your anxious brain is making it seem.
- **Focus on what you can control:** Anxiety thrives when we focus on things outside our control. Shift your attention to what you *can* control—your preparation, your attitude, your effort, and your approach to the situation.
- **Remember your past successes:** Think back to times when you've overcome challenges, big or small. Those wins are proof of your resilience and ability to adapt.
- **Get help:** Don't hesitate to reach out for support from a therapist, counselor, or support group. They can give you tools and strategies to better manage your anxiety.
- **Do 60 calf raises:** Stand up, go on your tiptoes, and come back down—do that 60 times. You'll use up your anxious energy and clear your mind. Plus, no one will even notice!

No one's saying bad things won't happen. But remember, bad things have happened before, and you made it through—probably even stronger than you realize. Anxiety will amplify everything to try to protect you, but it's an outdated mechanism that isn't serving you anymore.

Our goal is to be RESPONSIVE and not REACTIVE, which means we have to regulate our nervous system as anxious situations arise.

When we're more regulated, we can manage more than we think, be avoidant less, and live a richer, fuller life.

Life is not about waiting for the storm to pass,
it's about learning to dance in the rain.

— VIVIAN GREENE

FEELING YOUR ANXIETY WON'T KILL YOU, BUT AVOIDING IT JUST MIGHT.

3.

ENVIRONMENTS

YOU'RE NOT ANXIOUS; YOU'RE JUST LIVING IN AN ANXIOUS WORLD

As someone who's moved a lot in the past few years, I learned quickly that the city I lived in would influence me more than I could influence it. Our environments shape us in ways we can't control. I couldn't go to Los Angeles and make it care about anything beyond green juice and traffic. I couldn't ask New York to slow down, and I couldn't force my memories of Toronto to match my romanticized ideas of it when I'm homesick. The longer I stayed anywhere, the more it influenced me. My need to fit in caused a lot of anxiety, but since everyone else seemed to be fitting in fine, I thought I was the only anxious one.

I was wrong.

Imagine living in a house where all the lights are dim. The walls whisper worries, and the floor shakes with distant alarms you can hear but can't quite place. It's not exactly the most peaceful place to live, right? That's the vibe our world's been giving off lately, and it's triggering all our anxious feelings.

Stress levels are skyrocketing, and more people are seeing doctors for anxiety than ever before. This isn't a sign of weakness—it's our bodies reacting to the constant stress signals the world is throwing at us. Between late-night news blaring alerts, social media making us compare ourselves to strangers, and jobs that feel like endless hamster wheels, it's no wonder life feels like it's stomping on us.

What makes it worse is we blame ourselves for feeling anxious. We're led to believe it's our fault for not staying calm, even with all the chaos around us.

It's like yelling at a wilting houseplant for not thriving under your kitchen sink. You can water it all you want, but without sunlight, it's just waiting to die. The problem isn't the plant—it's the environment. Our mental health crisis isn't just about individual breakdowns; it's a giant alarm telling us the world is on fire.

> *You're not anxious, you're living appropriately given the conditions you're in.*
>
> — DR. JOANNA MACY

Feeling lonely when social media isolates you? Depressed in a job that drains your soul? Constantly anxious because the news is screaming about things you can't control? These are normal feelings in a world where anxiety is cranked up to the max. Add in a culture that glorifies sleep deprivation, substance abuse, and non-stop distractions, and we're all basically walking around like ticking time bombs of stress. We're constantly "on," stuck in a reality show where everyone's emotions are dialed up to 100, competing in a game we never signed up for. And guess what? There's no grand prize—just more drama.

You can scroll through self-help articles, meditate, or even read this book, but none of that will fix things if we keep ignoring the societal dumpster fire burning all around us.

The point isn't to give ourselves a free pass. **Healing requires taking some ownership of our suffering,** and with responsibility comes real power.* But it's also important to understand that our internal struggles often mirror what's happening around us. Just like a wilting houseplant needs more than a pep talk, we need an environment that nourishes our well-being instead of draining it.

That doesn't mean our personal efforts don't matter. Building resilience is like giving that wilting houseplant stronger roots. But even strong roots need fertile soil—a supportive community rather than one that isolates us. In a world obsessed with "every man for himself," it's no wonder we all feel so anxious.

Society often runs on the principle of least effort. We do just enough at our jobs to avoid trouble, knowing there's little point in going above and beyond because

* Fun fact: before Uncle Ben was giving cliché advice, he was selling rice with a problematic history.

no one would notice or care. This constant feeling of "not good enough" just piles more pressure onto our anxiety.

What makes it worse is that the system thrives on it. It feeds off the constant flow of fresh faces—young and hopeful—while it burns out the older, disillusioned ones. It's a vicious cycle, and our anxieties are both fuel for the system and a byproduct of the way it's built.

I haven't said anything funny in this chapter, and I'm still not going to, but I want to say there's light at the end of this anxiety tunnel.

Just because the game is rigged doesn't mean we can't change the rules. Sure, personal growth is an important first step, but to truly transform, we need a bigger shift—a change of scenery for us as a collective.

Grab that houseplant from under your sink now. Give it enough sunlight and fertile soil, surround it with other flourishing plants, and watch it bloom. Similarly, when we surround ourselves with kindness and communities that value compassion and connection, the anxious fog starts to lift. We relax, feel supported, and discover a resilience we didn't know we had.

Evolving ourselves is the first step to evolving the world. Our anxieties and anger don't just affect us—they contribute to the overall vibe around us. But when we choose kindness and stand up for what's right, we shift that vibe and make a difference.

This fight for a saner, kinder world isn't just a nice idea—it's about recognizing how our personal well-being is tied to the health of the world. It's about building real connections, supportive communities, and spaces where we can all thrive, not just for ourselves but for those around us.

We don't have to dance to the anxious music our world plays. We can change the tune—adding songs of compassion, connection, and action. Together, we can fix the broken parts of our world and create something brighter and more hopeful.

This is your life, and you deserve to feel amazing. While no one else is responsible for making you feel that way, understanding the environments you're in helps you create beauty within them. Just like you can absorb and add to the world's anxiety, you can also absorb and add to its beauty.

If you know anyone struggling with anxiety, share this message with them. Let's spread grace, love, and support, and see how much better the world can feel.

THE GROWING ANXIETY WE FEEL IS A SIGN THAT SOMETHING IS SERIOUSLY WRONG WITH THE WORLD, NOT US.

HUMBLE THE POET

4.

HABITS

ANXIETY'S BESTIES: GUILT & SHAME

I'm in the "overthink and be a perfectionist" stage of writing this book—that is, the book is done, and now I have a few weeks to go in with a fine-tooth comb and turn this from a good book to something amazing.

On the first day I was going to hunker down and start editing, a quick hi/bye stop at a Wednesday night birthday party turned into a late-night dance off. This was fine; I'd start the next day.

The next day, I get a call from a friend to join him and the boys for dinner a few blocks away. That dinner turns into a typical New York night.*

Then came the weekend.

It's safe to say I lost a week of being a perfectionist by being a complete degenerate.

I feel guilty about those types of choices. If I watch too much TV, or eat too much delicious food,** or sleep in, I feel absolutely wrecked and full of anxiety that I should be doing better. Then I often make even more unhelpful choices to cope with those anxious feelings.

We all have habits that might not be the most helpful—but notice I didn't call them bad habits. Judging them, or ourselves, harshly doesn't help. Our habits can both help and hurt us. In a world where everyone seems to have a perfect morning

* The highlight being exchanging Apple Music playlists with a stripper and not getting home until 2 PM the next day.

** Because we all know if it tastes good, it isn't good for you.

routine, run multiple businesses, find their soulmate, and travel on passive income, it's easy to feel like we're not good enough or doing the right things. Some of our habits might even make us feel ashamed. Wanting to improve ourselves is great, but **beating ourselves up over our choices doesn't help.**

Shame is like an annoying bird perched on our shoulder, squawking about everything we're doing wrong. The problem is, this bird never leaves—it just settles in and won't stop. And the more it squawks, the more we cling to those "bad" habits. Feeling ashamed for scrolling on our phones instead of working only makes us scroll more. We want to break free and change things, but guilt keeps us stuck, with the fear of failure hovering right behind it.

Since it's hard to say no to people, we often soften our refusals with passive and defeated excuses, saying things like, "I can't because. . ." instead of simply saying, "I won't." We create less anxiety and guilt when we replace "I can't" or "I have to" with assertive phrases like "I choose" or "I choose not to," giving us a sense of control and reducing shame in our responses.

Guilt and shame don't help us improve, they just make us tired and sad. You can't shame a caterpillar into becoming a butterfly faster. Growth happens on its own timeline, and pushing it with negativity only holds it back.

Most of us first felt guilt and shame from our parents. It's unfortunate they used these tools, but they had limited ways to help us and less emotional intelligence than we do now. As adults taking care of ourselves—and sometimes our kids—we need to remember that guilt and shame are not only harmful but also ineffective for long-term improvement. It's time to stop using them altogether.

Compassion and acceptance help us change bad habits more effectively than harsh self-criticism ever will. We know this because it's how we encourage others. Imagine treating yourself the way you help others—with love, patience, and compassion.

Think of yourself as your own inner toddler—would you scream at a three-year-old for accidentally spilling their juice? No. You'd offer them a cookie, maybe a hug, and say "Hey, we got this." That's the vibe we need.

To do this, we first have to acknowledge the shame we've felt. We need to name it and understand what it's whispering in our ear without letting it define us. We're not our habits; our habits are just chapters in our story.

Instead of beating ourselves up, let's be as kind to ourselves as we'd be to a child or a struggling friend. *Let's see our habits as symptoms, not sins.* Our less-than-ideal habits are often just coping mechanisms for unmet needs—whether it's comfort, escape, or a sense of safety. Some of us smoke because we're stressed, and then we get hooked on nicotine. The same goes for drinking, watching porn, or endlessly scrolling on our phones. The real problem is the stress, not the habit.

Now let's be honest with ourselves. Is the short-term relief of our unhelpful habit worth the long-term struggles? Are there more helpful alternatives we can try instead?

Healthier habits will only stick when we let go of trying to be perfect.

We can't solve all our problems in one day, but we can make progress. Small victories matter—the moments of awareness, the tiny steps toward change—they all count. Improving our habits without guilt and shame means focusing on progress, not perfection.

Sure, we all mess up—but there's no need to pile extra anxiety on top of that, like it's a tragic emotional sandwich no one ordered. *Our flaws make us human.* They make us vulnerable, and that's what allows us to connect with each other.

I'm writing this book because I struggle with these same things. If I was talking to you like I was perfect, this book would be unreadable. You'd have returned it, used it as kindling, or used it to fix a wobbly table a long time ago.

This is a journey; it's not a straight route or even a paved road. There will be setbacks, stumbles, and backtracks. That's part of what makes the journey worth taking.

Remember, *this isn't about becoming some idealized version of ourselves. It's about becoming our most authentic selves, flaws and all.* It's about embracing the messy, complex beauty of being human. It's about shedding the masks of shame and stepping into the light, unashamed, unafraid, and ready to dance to the rhythm of our own authentic self.

Guilt is a useless emotion.
It changes nothing of the past and only burdens the present.
— MAYA ANGELOU

There's no way reading one chapter in this book will end your life's situationship with guilt and shame, but we're making progress in the right direction. You had to feel it when you were young, but now that you're older, recognize when it's being used against you and the anxiety it causes, and focus on honoring who you really are before worrying about avoiding a guilt trip.

And for the love of all strippers and their amazing playlists, don't use guilt and shame on others. Let's break the cycle of using these as tools on ourselves and others.

YOU CAN'T SHAME A CATERPILLAR INTO BECOMING A BUTTERFLY FASTER.

HUMBLE THE POET

5.

REACTIONS

THE OVERTHINKING CRACKHEAD HAMSTER IN OUR HEAD

There's a hamster living in your head. He's addicted to energy drinks, and he salts the rim of the can with cocaine. You notice him most when you're struggling to sleep, because that's when this crackhead hamster is running on your mental hamster wheel, replaying the awkward comment you made at work, trying to figure out why they haven't texted back, and rehearsing every possible outcome for tomorrow's presentation. That hamster is overthinking, and this is our life with it bouncing off the walls of our mind, doing all the mental gymnastics, contorting every thought into a tangled knot of "what-ifs" and "maybes."

Overthinking doesn't actually help us solve problems—it just makes our survival brain believe that *the act of overthinking* is the solution.

Overthinking isn't just a quirky personality trait; it's something rooted deep in our brains. Much of our wiring comes from our hunter-gatherer ancestors, who were hardwired to be paranoid for their safety. It wasn't a safe time—there were no comforts, and constant threats meant staying alert was necessary for survival.

Overthinking has a negativity bias, an alarm system in our brains that constantly looks for, predicts, and exaggerates what's wrong. This alarm system once protected our ancestors from real dangers, like predators hiding in the bushes. Today, it makes us fear things like sending an embarrassing text or spilling coffee in public. What used to be a protective instinct is now an annoying inner critic, making us anxious even when there's no real danger.

In a physically dangerous world, being paranoid was useful, but in today's world of Wi-Fi, food delivery, and robot vacuums, it often works against us. Every harmless email feels threatening, and every social interaction seems full of judgment.

Our brain, which once protected us from danger, has now become one of the biggest threats to our peace of mind.

Dr. Kristen Neff, a self-compassion guru, describes overthinking as "the cruelest form of mental self-abuse." We've become our own worst enemies, replaying past conversations, analyzing facial expressions, and building walls of anxiety that have us avoiding new experiences and challenges.

Overthinking is pretending our intuition doesn't work—that gut feeling that whispers wisdom from deep inside us. It's like having a GPS in your car but ignoring it and asking a crackhead hamster for directions instead. That hamster will take you on a winding path of uncertainty and self-doubt.

Our intuition shows that we already know the answer, but we might not like it. So, we overthink to find another answer that feels better. Overthinking and ignoring our gut happen when we try to have too much control.

Viktor Frankl, a Holocaust survivor and psychiatrist, beautifully said, "Man cannot make his own fate, but he can choose how to cope with it."

Embracing life's uncertainties doesn't mean diving into chaos. It's about building resilience and adaptability. It's like dancing in the rain: you'll get wet, and that's okay. It's better than relying on a broken umbrella or avoiding the rain altogether. You learn to thrive even when things get messy.

We might not be able to completely stop overthinking and the anxiety it brings, but we can use practices to reduce its impact. We only overthink when we're not focused. When we focus on something, anything, that will help stop overthinking. Simple activities like doodling, counting breaths, or practicing mindfulness can keep us focused and prevent us from getting stuck in rumination.

Cognitive restructuring, which is just a fancy way of saying "reframing negativity," helps us fix the cracks in our self-esteem and replace them with kinder, more realistic views of ourselves.

Sometimes **the best way to avoid worrying is . . . to worry.**

Schedule a daily "worry break" to tame your anxieties. Think of it as a designated time for your worries to air out in a mental cage. Once the timer goes off, you lock them back in, freeing yourself to focus on the rest of your day without their constant chatter. This practice helps to manage anxious feelings by giving them a specific time and place, rather than letting them run wild all day.

In addition, the antidote to overthinking is a big, warm hug of self-acceptance. Let's choose to see mistakes as stepping stones, failures as learning opportunities, and overthinking as a temporary detour on the path to living fully.

The world will always be full of scary things that go bump in the night, but we don't need all the answers to dive into it. Sometimes, the greatest act of courage is just showing up, imperfections and all, and accepting the beautiful chaos of this journey.

I'm a professional overthinker and can find danger in a bouquet of flowers.* I'm always waiting for the other shoe to drop. I think I need to make all the right choices all the time, and the only way to do that is to have all the information. The problem is there's endless information, so instead I have analysis paralysis. This keeps me from doing anything, which is a form of protection and feeling in control. The problem with that is I don't make any growth or progress, just like that hamster on a wheel: running all day and never getting anywhere.

Instead of trying to make the RIGHT decision, let's make ANY decision, experience the consequences of that decision, and make more choices from those experiences. This is choosing trial and error over knowing the right answer ahead of time.**

Instead of being anxious crackhead hamsters on a wheel in our minds, we can hop off the wheel and be brave, yet flawed, explorers in the world. Make time for the "what-ifs" and keep it moving. It's completely okay to embrace the mess of life—it's what makes existing exciting. Let's dance, laugh, love, stumble, cry, and scream our way through this chaos of beauty. *The greatest things don't happen to people who ignore their doubts. They happen to those who learn to live despite them.*

Anxiety whispers, "What if you fail?" Hope says, "But what if you fly?"

— UNKNOWN

* Ninja bees.

** Reliable crystal balls are hard to come by these days.

OVERTHINKING
IS PRETENDING
OUR INTUITION
DOESN'T WORK.

DON'T LET THIS QR CODE FEEL LONELY

Scan it. Give it a purpose. Unlock the bonus chapters and make this little code's day.

PART 2:

EVERYDAY ANXIETY

6. ANXIOUS & NAKED IN PUBLIC

"I love how open-minded you are about things," Chris said, turning away from the window to look me in the eye as we rode the bus through Berlin.

I've known Chris since I was four, making him my longest-standing friend. We grew up across the street from each other and were in the same kindergarten and first-grade class. Although we didn't have the same teachers after that, we both became teachers. He even visited my class to do fun science experiments with my students.

Chris eventually moved to Germany to take a job at an international school. Years after losing contact, I made it out to Berlin to visit him. As we sat on the bus, I was confused about why he was praising my open-mindedness.

Chris asked if I wanted to join him at his favorite spa. Naturally, I said yes, thinking a relaxing massage was long overdue. But once I was fully committed and on the bus, he revealed we weren't going to a spa—at least not the kind I had imagined. We were headed to a European-style nude sauna.*

As he said it, I realized why he appreciated my openness. His compliment only reinforced the corner I'd painted myself into, and I was too proud to back out. We were about to get fully naked.

I had never been naked in front of any of my friends, nor had I seen them naked, let alone in a public space full of other naked people. As the bus approached our stop, my anxiety shot through the roof.

* I guess all those years in Germany had taken a toll on his English; he mixed up the words *spa* and *sauna*.

Unfamiliar, vulnerable, and downright strange experiences are bound to make us anxious because our survival brain doesn't know if they're safe or not. And to make things even more intense, I had taken an edible to enhance the massage I thought I was getting, so I was juggling multiple types of anxiety all at once.

Performance anxiety: Would I know how to act? Would people stare? What if I get caught staring?

Social anxiety: Is it normal to be naked in front of strangers and my oldest friend? Is it possible I'm going to be judged? Are any of my tattoos offensive in German?

Body image anxiety: What if people think I'm gross? I barely went to beaches, let alone complete nude saunas—what if my insecurity is written all over my face or my belly?

A lot of our anxiety comes from the fear of the unknown and the lack of safety it brings. But the truth is, we can't actually fear the unknown, because we wouldn't know what to fear. What we're really afraid of is what our survival brain projects into the unknown, based on past experiences. Our past hurt shapes our future fears.

Anxiety is our survival brain trying to prepare us for a threat, but it often fails to tell the difference between real danger and simply uncomfortable experiences. Sometimes, we only feel safe in public wearing baggy clothes because we're not comfortable with our body shape, without makeup, or when our beard isn't perfectly brushed.* It's about feeling secure, and new situations often take that feeling away because we don't yet have our bearings.

That's why we get nervous speaking to large crowds, going on first dates, or doing anything unfamiliar or vulnerable.

But that's life, and sometimes the only way to manage anxious feelings is to feel them and move forward anyway, allowing our survival brain to see that there was never really any threat in the first place.

I didn't share my anxieties with Chris, and maybe not wanting to let him down gave me the push I needed to step into this new experience. **We often act as the opposite of our fears,** so today, I decided to play the role of the confident,

* It's never perfectly brushed, my beard is untamable.

carefree guy who—despite not looking like an underwear model*—could still strut around naked with confidence. Surprisingly, the longer I did that, the calmer I felt.

By voluntarily stepping into this anxiety-inducing experience and allowing myself to feel all the emotions, I was showing my survival brain that there really wasn't any danger. This is how we train our brains to better understand when to sound the anxiety alarms and when to stay calm.

In the sauna, I noticed I wasn't the only one feeling self-conscious. Everyone seemed a bit uneasy—awkward postures, avoiding eye contact, and speaking a little too carefully. Most of us were first-timers, and our shared awkwardness actually made it a bit easier.

After about 30 minutes, I started to feel normal and adjusted, like I was in a society that never had clothes to begin with. But just as I was getting comfortable and my anxious alarms were fading, a new "threat" emerged, and those anxious feelings came rushing back.

There were kids.

Yes, kids. Whole-ass bare-ass nuclear families were at this sauna like it was a trip to the mall, complete with their naked kids running around, doing what kids do. I don't know if this sauna was special or my North American bias was showing, but it was a perfect example of how unexpected situations can suddenly trigger more anxiety.

Just like the initial anxiety, though, it started to fade with time and familiarity. We ended up spending a couple of hours at the sauna, exploring the different rooms, ice plunges, and relaxation areas before bundling up and heading back out into the Berlin winter.

Will I be running to another naked sauna experience anytime soon? Probably not. But did I have a great day that I'd have missed out on had I let my anxiety take over? Probably yes.

* I actually modeled for an underwear company a few years back. The pictures are online if you search the obvious keywords.

Chris also shared his anxiety about the situation, joking that I was the first guy in the group he saw naked, and it was an evolution in our friendship; the vulnerability made our bond a bit deeper.

Being seen is a tricky thing. We cover up more than just our bodies—we hide our true selves. **The anxiety isn't about who we are; it's about not knowing how others will react to us.** It's normal to feel scared and want to hide to protect ourselves, but that's not how we grow. Sometimes we just have to dive in, get used to the discomfort, and realize we're okay on the other side—even if we're wearing less clothes.

Let's revisit those anxieties:

Performance anxiety: I'm allowed to not know what to do in new situations and have fun learning and growing from figuring things out.

Social anxiety: It's not normal to be in these situations, but that's what makes them interesting. I can breathe through this, and I have the freedom and permission to leave at any time.

Body image anxiety: How often do I judge other people's bodies? It's natural to stare, and even if I had the sexiest body in the building, there aren't any prizes to be won.

OUR PAST HURTS
SHAPE OUR
FUTURE FEARS . . .

7.

ENVIRONMENTS

HOME IS WHERE THE ~~HEART IS~~ ANXIETY STARTS

Family is, well, family. We don't get to choose them, and growing up, they're all we knew, flaws and all. Our nature was shaped by our family, and as adults, it can feel like it takes forever to unlearn some of the patterns we picked up just by being around them.

Sometimes dealing with family feels like facing the ultimate boss in the video game of conquering anxiety. **They know how to push our buttons because they're the ones who installed them.** Family influences our anxiety from childhood, when we're most impressionable. The way we handle stress and anxiety as adults is often shaped by our early experiences at home. If we grew up in an environment where emotions weren't validated or conflicts were poorly managed, it's likely we'll struggle with anxiety later in life.

These early experiences often set the stage for our triggers as adults.

Many of us were told some version of "suck it up" or "stop being so sensitive," which led us to suppress our emotions and increase our anxiety. For those whose families avoided conflicts and ignored issues, we may feel anxious when facing situations where confrontation is needed.*

Family Drama

After a family member called me about some drama they were dealing with, I reached out to my sister. She gave me some bold advice: "Worry about yourself and your puppy; don't get sucked into their drama." Reducing anxiety often means

* Cue the music swell for the final boss battle.

building resilience, and that doesn't happen when we get caught up in drama and gossip that doesn't involve us.

Family drama and gossip can be big sources of anxiety. In some families, grudges, fights, and gossip are nonstop, creating a constant state of stress. Being around this kind of negativity is draining and makes it harder to handle the other challenges life throws at us.

Gossiping might seem fun at first,* but it eventually makes us feel unsafe and insecure, wondering what others might be saying about us behind our backs. It breaks down trust and creates a sense of paranoia, turning family gatherings into a minefield rather than a place of comfort and support.

People Pleasing Family Dynamics

Growing up, many of us learned to measure our value by how well we could appease others, especially those who were hard to please. Now, as adults, we might find ourselves stuck in people-pleasing cycles that fuel our anxiety and self-doubt. Recognizing where this need started can help us break free and build a healthier sense of self-worth.

If you have a parent who is overly critical or controlling, it can feel like nothing you do is ever good enough. This creates constant anxiety, where you try to please others and avoid conflict. Living in a home where every action is judged, achievements are downplayed, or emotions are dismissed can leave you on edge, even years later.

Dealing with these toxic behaviors is overwhelming and can affect other areas of your life, like relationships, work, and self-esteem. These toxic dynamics leave deep scars, some of which we don't even recognize until something triggers us later in life.

Studies have shown a strong link between growing up in a dysfunctional family and developing anxiety disorders as an adult.

Complex trauma happens in places where there isn't obvious abuse, but there is neglect, criticism, or emotional distance. This type of trauma, called complex PTSD (C-PTSD), usually comes from ongoing emotional neglect. Unlike a single traumatic event, complex trauma builds up over time, especially when we're kids. When we don't feel noticed or valued, it can lead to deep feelings of not being

* As a Punjabi, I love tea with my Cha.

good enough and anxiety that follow us into adulthood, making us rely on others' approval to feel okay about ourselves.

Even in families that aren't toxic or abusive, being around them can still cause anxiety. My family is great, but I struggle when I visit home. Going back sometimes brings up old versions of myself I'd rather forget*—like feeling insecure as a teenager or feeling invisible. Being home can trigger these old memories and anxieties, making it hard to relax.

Our families might also have expectations or beliefs that no longer match our own, which can make us feel isolated and anxious. We might feel misunderstood or pressured to fit in, even when we just want to be ourselves.

Boundaries with the Family

The key to managing anxiety around family is setting boundaries.

Daring to set boundaries is about
having the courage to love ourselves,
even when we risk disappointing others.

— BRENÉ BROWN

Boundaries, along with healthy habits like sleep, drinking water, minding our own business, having structure, and expressing ourselves, can greatly reduce anxiety from family interactions. They also help us understand how our families affect our feelings.

Some of you may still live at home and realize that **the rent-free life isn't really free—you're paying with your mental health.** If you're in a toxic family situation, save your money and find a way to move out. There's a lot of growth outside your bubble, and your resilience and ability to handle anxiety will improve.

Family dynamics can be tough and are often one of the hardest parts of reducing anxiety. Take it slow, be kind to yourself, and know that I'm right there with you. I moved to a whole different country and visit my family only a few times a year, and we actually get along.

* I made some questionable fashion and tattoo choices.

THE KEY TO MANAGING ANXIETY AROUND FAMILY IS SETTING BOUNDARIES.

8. CLASSROOMS & CUBICLES ARE FULL OF ANXIETY

If you think school or work is the problem, you're right—but it's not you, it's them.

School and work shape our routines, the people we spend time with, and even our self-esteem. No wonder they cause some of our worst anxiety. Whether you're a student or working in a corporate job, remember that these environments are relatively new to us as humans. This means they can easily trigger our brains to think we're in danger.

Deadlines and High Expectations

Remember that time you had 24 hours to complete a project that you had three weeks to do? Yeah, me neither, I always get stuff done ahead of time, like this book.*

Deadlines and high expectations are major anxiety triggers. In school, we juggle assignments, tests, and activities, while feeling pressure to do well from teachers, parents, and peers.

In the corporate world, deadlines and performance reviews create high stress. Employees feel constant pressure to prove their worth, meet targets, and climb the career ladder. This relentless pressure leads to burnout and anxiety.

A study linked feeling constantly rushed to higher levels of anxiety and depression. Our survival brain interprets constant busyness as a threat, causing anxiety. This response, useful for physical threats, only worsens school and work pressures.

* Don't be surprised if I turn up at your house while you're reading this to pencil in some more changes.

Acting Fake and Office Politics

If you ever wanted to win an Oscar, just act like you're interested in small talk with a co-worker who loves spreadsheets.

In both school and work, social fakeness and politics drain energy. In school, this includes cliques, peer pressure, and the need to fit in. Beyond schoolwork, students worry about being accepted and judged by others.

At work, office politics are even more complex. The need to network, navigate hierarchies, and maintain professional relationships makes us feel we have to be socially fake. This constant maneuvering is exhausting and that makes us more susceptible to anxious feelings. The social rejections we're avoiding become a danger, so we're more anxious about navigating these spaces.

Time and Energy Drains

Modern school and work setups drain our time and energy, reducing our resilience and making us more prone to anxiety. Long hours of studying or working leave little time for rest and self-care. Students stay up late to finish assignments and sacrifice enjoyment to study for exams. This lack of balance leads to chronic stress and anxiety.

For working folks, job demands, commuting, and personal responsibilities leave little room for relaxation. The constant hustle leads to physical and mental exhaustion. A two-week vacation once a year isn't enough; we're burning out because we're not doing enough of what matters.

These constant demands are seen as ongoing threats by our brain, keeping our stress response activated and causing prolonged anxiety.

Our Stone Age brains are trying to cope with a 21st-century world.

— ALICE BOYES

So, now that we know that school and work are pure gasoline for the fire of our anxious feelings, we should just quit everything and move into the jungles of Brazil to find the remaining tribes still living the way we're meant to live, right?

Well, you'll probably get anxiety from the lack of Wi-Fi there, but sure.

For the rest of us who want to keep life as-is but handle it better, here's the list of things within our power to improve how we feel when dealing with environments like school and work.

In addition to the usual suspects, to deal with anxious experiences in general:

- **Prioritize progress over perfection:** Doing a little better today/this week/this month than you did yesterday/last week/last month is more important than being perfect at school or your job.
- **Prioritize self-care to be more resilient:** Don't kill yourself for a class or a job that will replace you the moment you die. Take care of yourself like you're your own best friend. Call in sick, get the doctor's notes, take your vacation time.
- **Develop healthy boundaries with everybody and communicate them with love:** The nicest way to say no is "No."
- **Do things that make you present:** Be where your feet are, breathe, meditate, have great sex—life only matters when we're present in it.
- **Get outside help:** Great friends, great family, a great therapist, and even speaking to your dog can be places of support so you feel less isolated on this journey to reducing your school/work anxiety.

In addition to those things, my non-gospel, nonqualified, nonprofessional advice is this:

School: It isn't as serious as you think; a lot of people you meet in the real world aren't even making a living off what they did in school. Don't kill yourself during your youth, thinking it'll set you up as an adult. It may help you make some money and make your parents proud,* but if you're not happy with yourself, none of that matters.

Social skills and work ethic are the important parts of your education, and unless you're building things, fixing things, or need a license to practice it,** you can learn

* Proud here is defined as parents having one less thing to criticize you about.

** Doctor, lawyer, engineer—the immigrant child trifecta.

everything else on your own. I have very successful friends who went gray in their 20s so they could have high-paying careers. They're no more or less happy than my friends who work simple jobs; we all get used to our money and want more.

Work: **The trap isn't the job, it's the lifestyle you build around it.** With every bump in salary, we may bump up our lifestyle, and now we're trapped. You have to have an exit strategy to make working these jobs, and the stress that comes with them, worth it. Your boss will replace you the week after you get hit by a bus. Don't be overly loyal to your company. They're probably trying to figure out how to replace you with AI as we speak.*

Enjoy your existence, plan more fun, and realize vacations don't help with burnout. I have too many friends who played the game, kissed the asses, and bit their tongues, only to be furloughed in another round of cost-cutting. There's no safety and security in your job, so figure out how to be your own boss before that's the only option you have.

The goal of this whole book is to just make you more aware of what anxiety is, where it comes from, and what you can do about it, and our work/school lives are going to be one of the biggest chunks of it. It feels abusive how many people I meet are sinking in the bullshit of these institutions and thinking it's their fault. Life shouldn't be this intense, and you're not broken for being overwhelmed by it. We have to play the cards we're dealt, and I only hope this book helps you play it with a bigger smile.

* Wait, is my publisher trying to replace me with AI too?

LIFE SHOULDN'T BE THIS INTENSE, AND YOU'RE NOT BROKEN FOR BEING OVERWHELMED BY IT.

HUMBLE THE POET

9.

ENVIRONMENTS

ANXIOUS FRIENDS = ANXIOUS YOU

One of my proudest achievements in my journey as a dream chaser is that I haven't lost my friends along the way. I still have many of the same friends from elementary school, and now in our late 30s and early 40s, it's amazing that we're still close and haven't had much drama. We don't see each other as often as we used to, but that's just part of adult life. When I'm in town, we still get together for some last-minute plans. During the pandemic, we went on three-hour bike rides and treated ourselves to gas station chocolate bars and Gatorade. Poker games are still a regular thing, and the last time I visited, we hung out in a friend's backyard, trying to figure out the appeal of overpriced cigars.

That doesn't mean these are guys I'd instantly have connected with had we met as adults. Some of these guys are nuts, but they're my nuts and I love them.* My friends are a safe space for me and have impacted a lot of my behavior; sometimes that's a blessing, other times it's a curse.

Our friends and the company we keep affect our anxiety, so we need to choose them wisely.

Think about the times where one friend starts talking about how stressed they are about something, and before we know it, everyone in the group starts feeling anxious too, even if we weren't worried before.

The science behind this idea involves **mirror neurons**, a part of our brain that helps us connect with others. Discovered in Italy in the early 1990s, these neurons fire both when we do something and when we see someone else do the same

* I'm staying this confident even though they buy my books and don't read them.

thing. In other words, mirror neurons let us "mirror" the emotions and actions of people around us.

So, if your friend is feeling anxious, your mirror neurons can pick up on that stress and make you feel anxious too. This ability makes us more empathetic, but it also means we're more likely to absorb other people's anxiety.

The friends we choose can either help ease our anxiety or make it worse. Here are some ways our friends impact our mental health:

- **Positive influence:** Friends who are supportive, understanding, and calm can help us feel more relaxed and less anxious. They provide a safe space to share our worries and feel understood.
- **Negative influence:** On the other hand, friends who are always stressed, negative, or critical can increase our anxiety. Being around someone who expects the worst or puts us down can make us feel more anxious and insecure.
- **Peer pressure:** Friends can also affect our behavior in ways that add to anxiety. Feeling pressured to fit in or keep up with friends who do things we're uncomfortable with can cause a lot of stress.
- **Social comparison:** Comparing ourselves to our friends can lead to feeling inadequate, which increases anxiety. Constantly measuring our success, appearance, or achievements against others can hurt our self-esteem and raise anxiety levels.

Understanding how those around us impact our anxiety can help us make better choices about the company we keep. Here are some tips for building healthy, supportive friendships:

- **Seek positive relationships:** Surround yourself with people who uplift and support you. Friends who encourage you, listen to you, and make you feel valued can help reduce your anxiety.
- **Set boundaries:** It's okay to set boundaries with friends who are overly negative or stress you out. You don't have to cut them off completely, but it's important to protect your mental health by limiting your exposure to their negativity. Remember that setting boundaries isn't telling your friends who to be; it's teaching them how to be around you.

- **Communicate openly:** Honest communication is key to any healthy relationship. Let your friends know how you feel and what you need from them. This can help prevent misunderstandings and shrink anxiety.
- **Be a supportive friend:** Just as you want support from your friends, be there for them too. Building mutual support can strengthen your friendships and create a more positive environment for everyone.
- **Practice self-compassion:** The best friend you can have is yourself. Remind yourself that it's normal to feel anxious sometimes, and it's okay to seek help if you need it. Being kind to yourself and acknowledging your feelings can make it easier to manage anxiety.

It's totally fine to have different friends for different parts of your life. The friends I party with might not be the same ones I work with or get super vulnerable with. Figure out which friends fit best in different parts of your life, and let them thrive in those spaces. This might sound like putting people in boxes, but it's really about respecting the natural flow of our relationships. By letting friendships be what they are naturally, we avoid unrealistic expectations and potential disappointments. This way, each friend can be their authentic self, and your relationships can flourish where you connect best.

We need each other. Harvard research shows that loneliness and weak social connections can shorten our lifespan as much as smoking 15 cigarettes a day. Beyond individual friendships, being part of a supportive community will help reduce anxiety. Whether it's a school club, sports team, or online group, finding a community where you feel accepted as your authentic self can give you a sense of belonging and security.

It's not about having a ton of friends or being popular. A few close, supportive friends are much better for your mental health than a bunch of acquaintances. It's all about quality over quantity.

Some of the newer friends I've made on this journey are folks I see once a year or less. There are friends I love dearly but haven't seen in years, but I know when I do, we'll pick up right where we left off.

And don't forget to be a great friend to yourself. A strong relationship with yourself helps you be a great friend to others.

THE FRIENDS WE CHOOSE CAN EITHER HELP EASE OUR ANXIETY OR MAKE IT WORSE.

HUMBLE THE POET

10.

HABITS

OUR PHONES FEED ANXIETY

I've got two phones: the responsible one for everyday stuff and the cracked-screen chaos phone filled with social media, dating apps, fantasy football, and, of course, my cringy draft texts to exes that I swear I'll never send . . . again. The idea is that when I leave the house, I don't take that phone. So, I won't have access to all those distractions, and I'll barely look at the phone I take with me.

But I work from home, so both phones are often in both hands. Really, I just have two phones to split the endless doom-scrolling.

On top of that, on my main phone, I'm still in useless chat groups and reading click-bait news, pretending I'm keeping myself informed.

Technology used to exist to make our lives better; now it's switched to making our lives more convenient.* Our phones have a hypnotic glow, and we often reach for them without noticing.

I'm not sure when they changed from helpful little assistants to overbearing bosses who want to micromanage every waking moment of our lives, but it only seems to be getting worse.

Our phones make excellent servants, but over time, they have turned into horrible masters.

Life is lived through experiences. It's full of highs and lows, moments of joy and discomfort, and none of us makes it out alive. Through these moments, we learn, grow, and form connections that shape who we are. It's not always fun, but even

* There is a difference.

in tough times, we build resilience; discomfort builds strength. The problem with turning to our phones whenever we feel uncomfortable is that we're not only missing out on life experiences but also the strength needed to fully enjoy the journey of living.

In our hyperconnected, hyper convenient world, anything uncomfortable often feels like the enemy, leading to anxiety. But what if we saw these uncomfortable feelings not as something to avoid, but as signals, calls to action, or invitations to engage more fully with life? What if those anxious feelings are meant to be embraced because they help us grow—opportunities to push our boundaries and discover new strengths?

Sure, our phones keep us "connected." I now know what my second cousin ate for dinner, and I feel emotionally linked to my favorite influencer because I watched them cry into their morning smoothie. But more important than these "connections" is our connection with ourselves.

Connecting with ourselves means feeling discomfort in our bodies, thoughts, and emotions. Connecting with the vibrant, exciting, and often scary world means taking risks, being vulnerable, and accepting that things won't always feel wonderful. Embracing these moments can lead to significant personal growth and a more fulfilling life.

While our devices offer a temporary escape from life's anxieties, they also trap us in a passive state. We end up spending more time watching life through a screen instead of experiencing its raw, unfiltered beauty.

Thanks to technology, I can watch people cook an entire three-course meal and feel like I've achieved something. All while eating a bowl of cereal in bed. We're not forming our own experiences; we're just witnessing them and pretending to develop ourselves through them. Using our phones to avoid real life is like living in a bubble—safe, sure, but also boring as hell. Plus, no one ever grew as a person by binge-watching videos on their phone.*

Your phone is NOT your therapist. If mental health is a wound, your phone is the salt.

* Social media is curating our personalities to feel like predictable minimalist hipster coffee shops.

When's the last time you had a spontaneous conversation with a stranger* or sat on a bench and read a book?** Or felt the fear and thrill of trying something new? It's about stepping out of our comfort zones and into the unknown, embracing the uncertainty beyond the familiar.

Connecting with life means allowing ourselves to feel the full range of human emotions—joy, sorrow, fear, and excitement—that make life rich and beautiful. A life full of memories requires us to invite discomfort, pain, and confusion, despite the anxious feelings that come with them.

The stories where we come out on the other side of pain are the ones we tell with the most pride; those are the stories that make us interesting people.

> *We are constantly checking our phones*
> *because we are afraid of missing out on something.*
> *But what we are really missing out on is our own lives.*
>
> — CAL NEWPORT

If we spend 4 hours a day on our phone from the ages of 20 to 80, that adds up to 10 years of our life wasted on cat videos and rage-tweeting. That's years of life we could spend learning things we're interested in, spending time with people we care about, and making poor choices with hilarious consequences.***

Endless notifications, endless scrolling, and almost meaningless interactions online snooze some of our anxious feelings, but it's always temporary—and really expensive.

Devices give us dopamine; life gives us energy.

* And no, eavesdropping on a conversation while you pretend to scroll doesn't count.

** Hopefully you're doing it now with this one.

*** Like telling your friend how you really feel about his ex, only to watch them get back together a week later.

Our phones are our digital pacifiers.
We use them to soothe ourselves, to distract ourselves,
to escape from our own thoughts and feelings.

— DR. SHERRY TURKLE

Turning to digital devices gives us the illusion of spending time alone, but it does the opposite. Using our phones to escape actually increases our anxiety, creating a cycle of dependence and stress.

Constant connectivity, fear of missing out, and seeking artificial validation online leave us feeling inadequate. We compare ourselves to others and worry about their judgment even more. What was once a safe space has become a breeding ground for anxiety, making us addicted to it for temporary relief.

Breaking free from this requires real effort to disconnect from devices and reconnect with ourselves. It means shifting from seeking external validation to finding self-acceptance and inner peace. We need to face our anxieties rather than avoiding and numbing them through digital distractions. Digital soothing is not a substitute for managing our emotions.

My goal isn't to shame you for using your phone. **Scrolling on your phone is a completely normal response to how overwhelming life can be.** I do it all the time. A lot of what makes life overwhelming doesn't have an easy solution that you can control; the world is a mess, and you're not broken for feeling stressed about it. I'm not here to shame you, and I want to remind you not to shame yourself either. Being addicted to a device isn't something you can easily control. What you can manage is not being hard on yourself for it.

The journey beyond the screen isn't about throwing our phones down a sewer drain.* It's about reclaiming control over our relationship with it. *Let's look at technology as a tool, not as a crutch.* Let's set boundaries, create phone-free times and spaces in our lives, and prioritize smelly analog real-world experiences.

* That'll just lead to a bunch of phone-addicted Ninja Turtles.

Here are easy ways to do that immediately:

- Remove social media from the home screen, making it harder to find. One of my friends deletes the apps and reinstalls them each time he wants to use them.*
- There are apps that limit screen time. One such app is called Opal.
- Turn off ALL notifications and badges—yes, *all*.
- Change your phone color to grayscale. Color is a huge reason we get drawn in. I've been doing this for months, and whenever I turn the color back on, it burns my eyes. The colors on our phones are literally junk food for the eyes.
- Stop taking your phone everywhere you go.**

As we navigate this ever-growing digital world, remember that feeling better doesn't come from phone distractions but from building resilience. This means embracing a life full of challenges and uncertainties, understanding that these experiences help us grow, learn, and discover how rich life can be. When we choose to spend less time on our phones, we become stronger, more in tune with ourselves, and create more meaningful moments worth remembering.

* He has a few million followers and needs it for work, and he still does this.

** People survived in the 80s without phones in their pockets; so will you.

YOUR PHONE
IS NOT YOUR
THERAPIST.
IF MENTAL HEALTH
IS A WOUND,
YOUR PHONE
IS THE SALT.

HUMBLE THE POET

11.

HABITS

MULTITASKING ONLY MULTIPLIES ANXIETY

Normally I try to start these chapters off with a personal and sometimes funny story about my life, my beard, and all my unwise choices that amplify my anxious feelings, but in honor of this chapter on multitasking, I'm just going to focus on one thing: multitasking.*

Multitasking isn't real, and trying to do it makes you more anxious.

That's the chapter.

Now, if you're a die-hard multitasker and I've offended you, let's see if you can suck it up and keep reading.**

Let's quickly and simply break this down:

We all think we're super efficient ninjas, juggling a million things at once. It sounds great, especially since "busyness" is celebrated like a badge of honor. We treat multitasking like it's some glamorous superpower—like juggling flaming torches while riding a unicycle, reading this book, and knitting your cat a sweater, all without burning your apartment down. But **our brains aren't built to handle multiple tasks at once.** Yes, they're information superhighways but with only one lane. Trying to put two cars side-by-side on that narrow lane is bound to cause a spectacular accident.

* See what I did there?

** That counts as multitasking.

What we call multitasking is often just rapidly switching between tasks. True multitasking—doing several tasks at the same time—is a myth for the human brain, except for simple activities like walking and talking or patting your head while rubbing your belly.* When we "multitask," we're not giving each task our full attention, leading to a pile of unfinished tasks that can be overwhelming. Stanford professor Clifford Nass's research shows that multitasking reduces productivity and increases the likelihood of mistakes, especially for tasks that need focused attention and complex problem-solving.

On top of that, multitasking is the enemy of a regulated nervous system. When we multitask, our brains are constantly on high alert, scanning for the next thing to jump to. It's like having someone screaming "Switch!" every 0.5 seconds in your brain, keeping you on edge.

Every time we switch between tasks, our brain has to make a decision. That constant decision-making is draining our batteries. By the end of the day, we're left exhausted and unable to focus on anything.

Despite my fantastic points and citing research from smarter people than me, some of you still aren't convinced and treat multitasking as your love language. Hopefully my bearded voice will slowly slip into your brain as you begin to notice the endless and exhausting juggling between tasks.

When that moment happens, I won't say I told you so. I'll just leave you with these alternative strategies to getting things done without raising your anxiety in the process.

- **Make a battle plan:**** Write down all the things you need to do and pick the most important ones first.
- **Focus zones:** Block out chunks of time for each task and turn off distractions like your phone. It's like putting a "Do Not Disturb" sign on your brain—except this time, actually stick to it, unlike that vacation you said you'd "unplug" during.
- **Silence notifications:** Those constant pings and alerts are little thieves trying to steal your focus. Turn them off while you're working on a task.***

* Did you try it just now? Admit it, you did.

** That's just a sexier phrase for TO-DO LIST.

*** Or forever—you'll thank me later.

- **Train your brain:** Mindfulness exercises can help you train your brain to focus on the present moment and resist distractions. Think of it like brain boot camp for focus. My favorite mindful exercise is doodling butterflies with cool sunglasses.
- **Be kind to yourself:** Letting go of multitasking can be challenging. Start with small changes and celebrate your progress, no matter how small.

I actually wrote this chapter while rubbing my puppy's belly, cooking dinner, and watching the Toronto Maple Leafs once again get eliminated from the playoffs. So, I'm pretty much a multitasking wizard.* Don't be like the pretending-version of me. By prioritizing tasks and focusing on one at a time, you'll not only be more productive but also reduce anxiety and enhance your overall well-being.

I know I was a bit spicy with you in this chapter, and some of you feel personally attacked, so as an olive branch to mend our relationship, I'll share a joke.

What's the difference between a juggler and a multitasker?

Drumroll . . .

The juggler knows when to drop something.

Ba-dum tsssh.

* Or just a really audacious liar.

MULTITASKING ISN'T REAL—OUR BRAINS AREN'T BUILT FOR IT.

12.

HABITS

YOU ARE AS *ANXIOUS* AS WHAT YOU EAT

After months of the almighty algorithm sneakily slipping ads for a meal replacement shake into my feed, I finally spot it in real life at the grocery store,* like running into a celebrity. Except, this celebrity costs $6 and won't take a selfie. I decide that if this fills me up when I'm too busy to cook,** then it'll be worth it.

A few days later, I'm running late for an online meeting with a new creative partner, but I'm starving. I don't want my hanger*** to hurt the meeting, so I grab the shake and drink it while on the call.

The meeting goes great, and I decide to get some fresh-ish air**** and take the puppy out for a walk. As soon as I hit the street, though, I was slammed with a wave of overwhelm and anxiety. The cars seemed to honk louder, the sirens screamed, people rushed by faster than usual, and I couldn't get my bearings.

I've lived in this neighborhood for a year, and the hustle and bustle never bothered me like this before, but now my stomach was turning, and my body was shaking.

Then my brain went full detective mode: *Did that meeting secretly tank? But how could it? It was just an intro! Did I say something stupid? Was it my face? Was there a french fry in my beard?****** Why am I spiraling like this?*

* Advertising works.

** A.k.a too impatient to wait for the food to be delivered.

*** Hungry + angry.

**** That's the best we get in New York.

***** Again.

The shake!

I grabbed my phone like a caffeine-crazed detective, googling the brand name and "anxiety," only to find a gold mine of threads about people who lost their minds after downing that liquid panic attack in a bottle.

After a few hours, things went back to normal, and I realized my dream of $6 nutritious meals in a drinkable form was gone.

But there's something important to learn from this experience: **what we put in our body impacts how anxious we feel.**

Here's a nonexhaustive list of foods that might be fueling our anxiety. The goal here isn't to make you feel bad for eating these or to get you to clean out your fridge. It's just important to be aware of what may be affecting your mood and what might empower you to make changes if you want to feel better:

Caffeine: That cup of coffee or energy drink might seem like a pick-me-up, but caffeine can also make us feel like a squirrel on a sugar high, especially if we're already stressed.

Sugar: Sweet treats like candy, soda,* and pastries taste amazing, but that sugar rush is followed by a crash, leaving us feeling like deflated balloons.

Fake sugar: Some studies suggest artificial sweeteners mess with our mood and anxiety, like a sweet-tasting Trojan horse.

Processed food: Your favorite chips and frozen meals are like edible couch potatoes—deliciously useless. They weigh you down and zap your brainpower like a Netflix binge, but without the satisfaction.

High-glycemic carbohydrates: White bread, pastries, and other highly processed carbs cause quick spikes and drops in blood sugar levels, turning us into emotional rollercoasters.

Fried foods: Delicious, yes. But high in trans fats, these bad boys are like deep-frying your own mood—crispy on the outside, but greasy chaos inside.

* Pop for my fellow Canucks.

Dairy: For those who are lactose intolerant or sensitive to milk proteins, dairy can trigger inflammation and mood changes. It's like your body saying, "No cheese for you!"

Spicy food: Delicious, but for some people, spicy foods can trigger digestive issues that can make anxiety symptoms worse. If spicy dishes make your stomach feel like a crappy CGI dragon from GoT, maybe dial it back a notch.

Alcohol: While a drink might seem relaxing at first, alcohol is actually a depressant that can make anxiety worse in the long run. Sure, it feels like a warm hug at the moment, but it's more like a hug from a friend who talks behind your back—comforting for a second, but it'll mess you up later.

Also, *how much* we eat impacts how we feel.

- **Big meals:** Eating a huge meal might seem comforting, but it can also leave you feeling sluggish and uncomfortable, which can contribute to anxiety. Think smaller, more frequent meals to keep your energy levels stable.
- **Skipping meals:** When we skip meals, our blood sugar levels drop, which can make us feel grumpy and stressed. It's like our brain is a car that runs out of gas—it starts to sputter and can't function right.
- **Not enough water:** Water is essential for keeping our bodies running smoothly. Not drinking enough can leave us feeling off. Dehydration can make it hard to focus and can even affect our mood, and most of us don't realize when we're dehydrated.

Often, when we feel anxious, we want to run and curl up into a safe and comfortable space, and sometimes that comfort shows up as anxious eating. Anxious eating is like regular eating's emotionally unstable cousin—it's fueled by feelings, not actual hunger.

Food becomes a distraction from the things stressing us out, temporarily easing the discomfort. When we're stressed, our body releases cortisol, which can increase our appetite and make us crave sugary, fatty, or salty foods. Those foods trigger the release of feel-good chemicals, like endorphins, providing short-term comfort. But while it may soothe us for a moment, it doesn't address the root of the anxiety.

Over time, anxious eating becomes a habit. So, when we feel anxious, we automatically reach for food, even if we're not really hungry.

This can become a problem; because we're not making the best food choices, we can end up feeling guilty about those choices, which itself deepens our anxious feelings even more.

So how do we address the anxious eating?

- **Identify the triggers:** What situations or feelings make you want to reach for food?
- **Better coping mechanisms:** Find more helpful ways to manage anxiety, like exercise, relaxation techniques, or talking to a friend.
- **Mindful eating:** Pay attention to your body's hunger cues. Eat slowly and savor your food—like you're some kind of fancy food critic instead of a distracted TV snacker who forgets they're on their third bag of chips. This is tough for me, since I love eating in front of the TV, which makes it even harder to notice what and how much I'm eating.
- **Don't restrict:** Depriving yourself can lead to cravings and binge eating. Focus on balanced meals and healthy snacks. The goal isn't to be on some temporary miracle diet; it's to have a regularly balanced diet that you can eat forever without having to rely on intense discipline to do it.

Many of us struggle with anxious eating, making poor food choices, and not realizing how what we eat can affect how we feel. I'll still indulge in all the foods on the naughty list and probably make poor choices while doing it, but at least now I know how they'll make me feel. So, I won't be anxious about feeling anxious when it happens.

A food cheat code is protein. Protein helps keep blood sugar steady, which can prevent mood swings that fuel anxiety. Try adding protein to each meal—even a handful of nuts or a yogurt can help you feel more grounded when anxiety hits.

Instead of relying on $6 meal replacements, I'm back to splurging on takeout because apparently there are no other options.[*] I'm grateful for the experience, though, because it made me pay attention to how food impacts me emotionally, not just how full I feel. The more aware we are, the more empowered we become to make small choices that lead to feeling better in our lives.

What we eat decides how we feel. If you want to explore how our gut health impacts our anxiety, scan the QR code for a bonus chapter: PROTECT YOUR GUT.

* I can't cook because I'm using my oven to store my winter clothes.

WHAT WE PUT
IN OUR BODY
IMPACTS HOW
ANXIOUS WE FEEL.

THIS PAGE WAS FEELING EMPTY, SO WE ADDED A QR CODE

Scan it to fill the void (in the page and maybe in your soul?) with some bonus chapters.

PART 3:

BREAKING ANXIOUS PATTERNS

13.

REACTIONS

STOP AVOIDING YOUR TRIGGERS

Often when we're asked, "What's your biggest regret?" we respond philosophically, suggesting that we shouldn't have regrets since everything we've done has shaped who we are today. We learn from our mistakes, and since we don't have a time machine, dwelling on regrets seems pointless.

But honestly, I do have one big regret, and if I'm being real, it might be my only regret.

I regret how I handled putting my first dog, Himmatt, to sleep.

He had lost the use of both his hips and couldn't walk. It was clear that his time was coming to an end, and while I don't regret the decision to put him to rest, I heavily regret how we did it.

We took him to his vet, who, in hindsight, seemed less than empathetic about the whole thing. For him, it was just another day at the office. Himmatt looked at me, crying the whole time, wanting to leave, wanting to go home—scared and confused, lying on top of a cold, sterilized steel table. Those were his final moments.

If I could do it all over again, I would've found a veterinarian who could come to our house. We could've fed him everything he loved and quietly given him the needle, allowing him to drift off slowly in the home he grew up in.

I'll forever feel like a piece of shit for that.

Sure, I can practice self-compassion and remind myself that in the emotional hurricane I was going through at the time, a house call didn't even cross my mind. But that's not enough to ease my pain, and it's hard to think about it without tearing up.

Like most traumatic moments, my brain shoved it deep into the back of my mind, hiding it away—until something brought it all rushing back.

Over a decade later, about a year into having my new puppy, Boogie, the world had finally opened up after the pandemic, and it was our first in-person visit to her vet. Before that, I'd drop her off and pick her up at the front door. But now in LA, things were open, and it was time to get Boogie some vaccinations.

When we walked into the examination room, I almost threw up. There it was, the cold, sanitized, steel table, and this time, my new baby was lying on it, looking up at me to save her.

I was triggered.

A trigger is like a cue or signal that reminds your brain of something from the past. It can be tied to something good or bad, but we usually think of triggers in terms of stress or negative experiences. When your brain spots a trigger, it can set off a stress response, even if there's no real danger right now.

- **A Sound:** If you were in a car crash with a loud bang, you might feel anxious when you hear a sudden, loud noise again.
- **A Smell:** A specific perfume might remind you of a loved one who's passed away, bringing up feelings of sadness.
- **A Place:** Being in a certain room or location might remind you of a past trauma, like a robbery or assault.
- **A Word or Phrase:** Hearing a particular word or phrase might bring up strong negative feelings or memories, like anger or shame.

A trigger is our survival brain bracing for impact, even when no danger exists. Your brain is just trying to protect you based on what's happened before.

When we face a trigger, it's like our brain hits the panic button based on past experiences. That steel table? To my survival brain, it wasn't just metal and cold—it was a signal of danger because it reminded me of a painful memory. It's like my brain said, "Oh no, this again!" and started bracing for impact, even though the situation wasn't dangerous now.

Our survival brain is always on the lookout for patterns from the past to keep us safe, so when something reminds it of a tough time, it reacts as if the threat is happening all over again. It's trying to protect us, but sometimes that protection feels more like an overreaction.

Dr. Lisa Feldman Barrett, an expert in emotions, supports this idea. In her book *How Emotions Are Made*, she explains that our brains use past experiences to predict our feelings and reactions. It's like our brain has its own algorithm, serving up emotions based on what we've seen before—except this algorithm isn't as fun as binge-watching a new show served up by our social media feed.

When we're triggered, it's not about facing real danger—it's more about our brain saying, "This feels like danger." Think of your survival brain as an underqualified fortune teller trying to guess what's coming based on past stuff. It's not magic; it just makes everything feel like a bigger deal than it might be.

Understanding this can be a game-changer. Our nervous system isn't just reacting; it's guessing and preparing for chaos, even when everything seems calm.

If we're serious about healing and feeling better, we need to recognize that triggers show us where the wounds are.

These reactions can show us where our brain might be overreacting. Instead of ignoring or brushing off these triggers, try facing them. Yes, my friends, **stop avoiding your triggers.** By exploring them with curiosity, not judgment, we can understand what's really driving our anxiety. And using self-regulation techniques during chaotic times can help us stay calm when new challenges pop up.

When we let ourselves feel our triggers, experiencing and identifying them for what they are, dealing with them gets easier. They can even help us in the following ways:

- **Spotting Patterns:** Triggers help us see where our brain's trying to protect us based on old experiences. Recognizing these patterns shows us why we react the way we do.
- **Understanding the Cause:** By digging into our triggers, we can trace them back to the original experiences that started our reactions. This helps us tackle the deeper anxieties.
- **Changing Predictions:** Knowing our triggers lets us work on changing how our brain predicts what will happen next.

Keep in mind, triggers didn't show up overnight, and they won't go away instantly. Building new patterns takes time, so be patient with yourself and celebrate the small wins. Everyone experiences triggers—they don't define who we are or how strong we are. Great ways to tackle triggers and turn them into chances for growth include:

- **Mindfulness:** Staying present helps manage anxiety. By focusing on the here and now and observing your thoughts and feelings without getting tangled up in them, triggers won't feel as overwhelming.
- **Cognitive Behavioral Therapy (CBT):** CBT can change those negative thinking patterns. If you often think you'll mess up in social situations, CBT helps you replace those thoughts with more positive and realistic ones.
- **Exposure Therapy:** Facing your fears gradually can show your brain that what scares you isn't actually that bad. For example, if public speaking makes you anxious, practicing it little by little can help your brain realize it's manageable.
- **Self-Compassion:** Be kind to yourself when you're triggered. These reactions are just your survival brain's way of trying to protect you. Treating yourself with compassion can make triggers less intense and help you bounce back faster.
- **Organization and Calm:** Your surroundings play a big role in how you react to triggers. A cluttered workspace, loud noises, or certain smells can ramp up anxiety. Keeping your environment calm and organized can help reduce these triggers.

Using these strategies can make dealing with triggers less daunting and help you rewrite those anxious predictions.

Which brings us to finding balance. As a society, we often swing between saying "Don't be so sensitive," and "Don't trigger me," but neither of these really helps. What we need is a balance between seeking comfort and facing our triggers.

Comfort zones are like a cozy blanket—they make us feel secure and help us recharge, especially if we face a lot of negativity or stress. But **while it's great to have these moments of rest, we shouldn't use them to completely avoid our triggers.**

Facing triggers with the right support is like giving our minds a tune-up. It helps us deal with past experiences and build up our resilience. So, use those moments of comfort to recharge, but also try to gradually face your triggers. Each step forward makes you a bit stronger.

Think of triggers as our brain passing along info. **Each trigger is a little clue about past hurts and things we haven't fully worked through.** When we're in a better headspace, revisiting these moments can help us break patterns that aren't serving us anymore. Facing our triggers and understanding how our brain makes predictions can actually help us handle anxiety better. When something triggers us, it's our brain's way of saying, "Hey, we might need to rethink this." By dealing with these triggers directly and paying attention to them, we can spot old patterns and work on creating new, healthier ones. This way, we not only manage anxiety more effectively but also build our emotional strength and well-being.

A month ago, Boogie's groomer told me she needed updated shots before her next haircut.* This meant another trip to the vet. As soon as we entered the building, I felt my body tense up. I knew a trigger was forming because my body remembered that shiny steel table behind the next door. Instead of avoiding it, I faced it. I gave myself a gentle pep talk, took some deep breaths, and slowly walked into the exam room.

The anxiety was still there, simmering like a pot of pasta left on the stove, but it was manageable, and more importantly, I understood why it was happening, which kept it from boiling over. I had lost someone incredibly important on a table like that, so I don't blame my body for sensing danger. It's going to take more visits for my brain to stop flashing back to the saddest day of my life when I see that table, but I'm ready. I'm willing to dive into that pain and face those memories, so when Boogie looks up at me in fear, I can smile back, knowing it's just 15 tough minutes that end with her getting more treats than she can handle.

I'm not here to make all your triggers go away—I'm here to help you understand them better. With love, I encourage you to lean in to them, so you're not avoiding important parts of your life. And when new triggers form, you can address them at the root even earlier. So the next time our brain asks, "What does this remind me of?" our answer isn't "DANGER!" but instead, "An uncomfortable memory—that's an invitation to grow."

---

* Ungroomed goldendoodles look like they fell off the wagon and back on the bottle.

FACING TRIGGERS ISN'T ABOUT ERASING PAIN; IT'S ABOUT UNDERSTANDING IT BETTER.

HUMBLE THE POET

14.

THOUGHTS

OVERACHIEVERS ARE OVERANXIOUS

Often **it's not when things go wrong that we get anxiety, but when things go right.** In 2010, my song "Baagi Music" hit a million views. The praise came in, comments stacked up, the numbers grew, and opportunities started to appear. You'd think I'd be on cloud nine, right? Nope, I was stressed out of my mind.

After years of grinding, this "overnight success" felt like a tidal wave. Suddenly, I doubted myself, thinking, "You just got lucky; this won't happen again." The pressure to make another hit was crushing. A big-shot music lawyer in NYC even told me I'd be irrelevant without another hit, planting a seed of anxiety that spread like wildfire.

Instead of enjoying the success, I was paralyzed by the fear of not living up to it. The joy of making music turned into dread over meeting expectations. Eventually, I went the other way and stopped trying to make hit music at all. I'd love to say I did this to choose peace over pressure, but really, the chase was so overwhelming that I just gave up.

This taught me that overachieving can be a double-edged sword. **The higher we climb, the more we worry about falling—or at least that's what our anxious minds tell us.** The real trick is finding harmony between ambition and well-being, celebrating our wins without letting the fear of future flops take over.

You don't have to be an artist to relate to this. When we're stuck in a cycle of achievement, with trophies on the shelf and straight A's on the report card, we start to define ourselves by those successes. Compliments can start to backfire because they add pressure to keep achieving just to keep up that image.

This is the overachiever's paradox. We wear ambition like armor, constantly pushing for more, but it's often anxiety driving us. It's a familiar story: **the anxiety of overachieving comes from a mix of praise, pressure, and a fear of failing.** We end up tying our self-worth to our wins and other people's approval. And even though failure is a part of growth, every misstep feels like a punch to the gut, making us question our value and feel like impostors.

> *Most successful people are just a walking anxiety disorder harnessed for productivity.*
>
> — ANDREW WILKINSON

We overanalyze every project, worry about failing in the future, and push ourselves harder, always chasing a goal that keeps moving. At first, we crave the praise, the wins, and the rewards. But then our expectations shift. Suddenly, doing something that might be life-changing for someone else just feels like the bare minimum to keep ourselves afloat.

Success isn't a finish line—it's a moving target that fuels anxiety when we tie our self-worth to it.

A lot of this goes back to childhood. Early praise for good grades can mess with how we see ourselves. Instead of thinking intelligence is something we can grow, we start to believe we were just born smart. So, when we fail, it feels like we're betraying that image. We end up trapped by our own reputation, mistaking the walls of that trap for something impressive to show off to the world.

This need to be flawless is a mask we wear to meet people's invisible expectations, and it fuels our anxiety. It makes us procrastinate because we're scared of falling short and not living up to the impossible standards we've set for ourselves.

But here's the truth we all* need to hear: being good, smart, talented, or amazing isn't some fixed label. It's a journey of learning and growing. Mistakes aren't failures—they're part of the process, showing that we're pushing ourselves beyond what's comfortable.

* Including me.

And the real kicker? Our worth isn't tied to achievements or praise—and if it is, we might want to cut that cord before it turns into a leash. We can't measure our value in gold stars or compliments, and **chasing outside validation keeps us from building real self-respect.**

How We Cope

Right now, we subconsciously tell ourselves that as long as we keep winning, we're okay, and there's something appealing about overachieving. Society loves that we're productivity machines, and hustle culture tells us to "sleep when we're dead." We believe all our anxiety will disappear once we get over the next hurdle, but these hurdles are based on the stories we create. I keep telling myself that life will get easier once the first draft of this book is done, but this isn't my first rodeo. There are still a million things to do after the book is finished.

How We Could Cope Better

What we* need to realize is that the journey is all we have, and constantly chasing achievements has no real value. This starts with awareness. Pick up on the patterns, the internal critic whispering doubts, and the suffocating grip of trying to be perfect all the time. *Let's let go of who we think we should be and embrace who we truly are.* This requires self-compassion, replacing harsh self-criticism with kindness and understanding.

- **Overachieving me (destination-focused):** *It's been three days and you haven't worked on the book. You're going to miss your deadline, and everything will crash and burn, plus what you already wrote is trash. We'll never get this book done.*
- **Self-compassionate me (journey-focused):** *We haven't written in a few days. Is it because we're tired or scared of something? This used to be a lot of fun. What's changed? How can we spend our time off to get our battery charged? What small things can we do today to help keep us on track and enjoying this journey?*

* Especially myself.

We're all works in progress, and that's okay.

We all stumble, fail, and need to take breaks. That's okay.

Rest and relaxation aren't rewards we get after achieving something; they're essential for taking care of ourselves—mentally, physically, and spiritually. Taking breaks from constant work lets us recharge, look at our goals with fresh eyes, and remember why we love what we do.

I'm not asking you to let go of your ambition—I love pushing myself and reaching my potential—but it's only sustainable when done for the *joy* of the journey, not out of *fear* of failure. Focus on the fun of learning, growing, and becoming the best version of yourself, and **let go of the idea that you need to be some perfect version of someone you never wanted to be.**

We all experience anxiety, doubt, and fear of failure, but we also share resilience, determination, and the ability to achieve great things. So, take a deep breath, fellow overachiever, and let go of the anxieties that drive you. Instead, focus on your true potential. The world needs you, with all your flaws, free from the unrealistic expectations you set for yourself long ago.

Let's not be prisoners of our past labels; let's be explorers of our own possibilities. Thinking we can outwork our anxieties will only leave us burned out and feeling worse about ourselves. Have some fun and see what comes from it.

In 2017, I released another EP of music, and my song "H.A.I.R." became an organic labor of love that turned into my most popular song, even surpassing the success of "Baagi Music." Ironically, just a month later, my first book *UnLearn* took off, and my adventures as an author began, pushing music to the back burner once again. After this book is finished, I hope to spend more time in the studio—not to keep my music side relevant but to continue enjoying that part of my creativity and have fun.

LET'S NOT BE PRISONERS OF OUR PAST LABELS; LET'S BE EXPLORERS OF OUR OWN POSSIBILITIES.

HUMBLE THE POET

15.

THOUGHTS

DON'T "SHOULD" ALL OVER YOURSELF

- "I should be more productive."
- "I should be happier."
- "I should have figured this out by now."
- "I should look a certain way."
- "I should be further along in life."
- "I should be able to handle this on my own."
- "I should always be there for everyone."
- "I should never make mistakes."
- "I should be in a relationship by now."
- "I should always be calm and composed."
- "I should know what I want to do with my life."
- "I should always be positive."

We're *"should-ing"* ourselves to an anxious death.

Every time we use the word *should*, we set another unrealistic expectation that feeds our anxiety. These "shoulds" make us feel pressured, not good enough, and constantly judged. If you want to feel less anxious, you need to remove the word *should* from your vocabulary. Social media is full of people telling us what we should do. Society is full of expectations of who we "should" be. Culture, religion, and tradition are all shoulding all over us, triggering our anxiety to endless levels.

I, like you, am "shoulding" on myself all the time. I get trapped thinking about invisible milestones and outside expectations, stressing myself out, always focusing on what I SHOULD be doing. I'm unmarried and childless* in my 40s. Sometimes I feel liberated; other times I feel like I should be living my life another way. Sometimes I feel like I should be at the gym more. I should be investing more. I should be brushing my beard more. It's an endless cycle that only heightens my anxious feelings.

"Should" statements are the emperors of the land of "never good enough."

— MARIANNE WILLIAMSON

Using the word *should* tricks our survival brain, the amygdala, into thinking unrealistic expectations are threats and dangers. Studies by Dr. Rick Hanson, a neuropsychologist, explains how certain thought patterns like chronic "should" thinking can keep us in a perpetual state of anxiety, as if we're constantly under threat. This puts us in a constant state of fight-or-flight, making anxiety a constant companion.

Even though the word itself looks and sounds harmless, it's a grenade loaded with anxious ideas, just waiting to explode. Using and thinking the word *should* leads to anxious feelings in a few ways.

- **Unrealistic expectations:** "Shoulds" compare us to an ideal but not realistic version of ourselves; that sets us up for comparison, failure, and disappointment. Our amygdala interprets this as a threat, slamming the big anxiety alarm button.
- **Guilt and shame:** The stress hormones released from not meeting our unrealistic expectations feed the guilt-shame cycle. We're anxious, and that makes us guilty and ashamed, and feeling guilt and shame further worsens anxious feelings.
- **Focus on the negative:** When we use the word *should*, we're focusing on what we lack, stealing our ability to stay present and enjoy the moment. This makes us anxious about the future.

* I think.

Unfortunately, the solution isn't simply banning the word from your vocabulary. We'll still have thoughts and constant triggers around us for how we and others should be. Instead, here are a few strategies for when we find ourselves in a *should* spiral:

- **Challenge the *should*:** Let's ask ourselves, "Is this 'should' really helpful, or is it just making me anxious?" Questioning the "should" disrupts its impact to trigger our amygdala and reduces how much anxiety alarms get triggered.
- **Reframe with a *could/might*:** A simple switch from *s* to *c* can make all the difference. Instead of "should," try "I could" or "I might." This empowers us and opens possibilities. Having possibilities reduces despair and has us feeling less triggered.

  For example, "I should be more productive" becomes "I could focus on one task at a time." "I should be happier" becomes "I could do more things that bring me joy."

  Even when we hit ourselves with the "coulds," let's follow them up with "and that's okay." For example, "Instead of playing video games, I COULD be finishing this book. And that's okay."
- **Focus on values:** Knowing what actually and uniquely matters to us eliminates a gang of shoulds from our lives. Knowing our core values lets us align our actions with our values instead of defaulting to societal expectations.
- **Self-compassion:** Everyone makes mistakes. Let's be kind to ourselves instead of adding guilt to the mix. Self-compassion lets the amygdala rest and elevates a sense of calm.

Should is the cousin of perfectionism, which itself is a made-up idea because no one is perfect.

Perfectionism isn't about doing things perfectly; it's about finding faults easily.

> *Perfectionism is self-destructive simply*
> *because perfection doesn't exist.*
> *It's an unattainable goal.*
>
> — BRENÉ BROWN

Having grace with ourselves and being kinder isn't just about doing a good thing; it's directly linked to keeping our nervous system more prepared and regulated. The less we're triggered by imaginary threats, the better prepared we are for the real ones, and the calmer we'll feel throughout the day.

Letting go of the "shoulds" means focusing on our own progress instead of trying to appear perfect for everyone else. It's a reminder that we're not here to compete or be compared to others, and everyone's journey is their own. By doing this and focusing on what truly matters to us, we can reduce our anxious feelings and live a life that feels much better.

Now I sh. . . *could* go to bed, as it's past midnight, but I'll probably play another round of Fifa before. And that's okay.*

Lastly I want to thank my friend Phil Nosworthy for inspiring this chapter and granting me his valuable time monthly to help energize, inspire, and help me be a better person.

* 😉

PERFECTIONISM ISN'T ABOUT DOING THINGS PERFECTLY; IT'S ABOUT FINDING FAULTS EASILY.

HUMBLE THE POET

16.

REACTIONS

THERE'S ANXIETY HIDING BEHIND THAT TEMPER

Since the day I got my pup, she's been my shadow, following me everywhere. I walk her off-leash through the city, but we started small and worked our way up—from empty parks to sidewalks without street crossings. It didn't take long to teach her to stay off the curb. Now she's a pro. We wander NYC together, turning heads and drawing admiration from dog owners and tourists alike.

One day, an older man walking his dog decided to say, "In America, we walk our dogs on a leash; it's the law."* The leash comment was one thing, but bringing up the United States felt off—as the Zoomers would say, "It's giving racism." I had two choices: ignore him or have some dramatic fun. I chose the latter and asked him to repeat himself, but he just awkwardly sped up and walked away.

Later that week a friend said to me, "Bro put your dog on a leash. It's giving me anxiety," and I made a connection. Were both comments inspired by that same anxiety?

One inconvenient truth I've learned while writing this book is how much empathy we need to show to people who act like jerks. Often these people are among the most anxious and have the least healthy coping mechanisms.

Now I can't unsee it. Whenever I encounter someone who's rude, aggressive, or snobby, I see a scared, anxious child inside them. Seeing this helps me understand the scared, anxious child in me too.

* Funnily enough, I once got out of a traffic ticket in LA shrugging to the police officer and saying, "Sorry, I'm Canadian."

Just like animals attack when they feel threatened, we do the same. **Anger is often a mask for anxiety,** triggered when our survival brain senses danger. These threats can range from something as random as a flying squirrel to someone being rude to us. Our brain responds by flooding us with cortisol and adrenaline, chemicals that prepare us to fight or flee. But instead of running or fighting, sometimes we end up yelling at an unlucky customer service person.

Understanding this doesn't excuse bad behavior, but it does help us respond with empathy instead of making things worse. Expressing anger can temporarily relieve anxiety, so we lash out instead of addressing the underlying issues. This creates a cycle where anxiety feeds anger, and anger feeds anxiety, leaving us stuck and frustrated.

Anxiety can lead to anger when worry becomes too much and makes us irritable, while anger can lead to anxiety when we're concerned about the fallout from our outbursts.

Understanding what triggers our anger can reveal the root of some of our anxiety. Everyone has different triggers that can set off anger and anxiety:

- **Stress:** High levels of stress make us more prone to both anxiety and anger. When we're stressed, it's easier to react angrily to minor things.
- **Frustration:** When things don't go as planned or we face obstacles, it frustrates us, which can quickly turn into anger.
- **Fear and insecurity:** Feeling afraid or insecure makes us more likely to lash out in anger as a way to protect ourselves.
- **Past experiences:** Past experiences of hurt or betrayal make us more sensitive to similar situations, triggering anger and anxiety.

A lot of the emotions tied to our triggers are tough to identify or express, so we push them down and use anger as an outlet. We might snap at our partner because we feel insecure about the relationship, or argue with a friend because we're secretly afraid of being wrong. If we don't confront these deeper feelings, our anger will keep bubbling up.

When we're triggered, anger often kicks in automatically because our survival brain reacts instantly. This happens before our logical brain has a chance to take control.

Knowing this helps us understand why we might lash out and gives us a better chance to manage our reactions.

Unchecked anger has a big impact on our lives. It damages relationships, harms our health, and can even hurt our careers. Studies have shown a link between chronic anger and high blood pressure, heart disease, and even depression.

We're not powerless against anger, but that doesn't mean we can simply stop reacting. Instead, we have to see anger as a first *reaction* that we have to get under control and replace it with a useful *response* that can improve the situation. *Responding > Reacting*

In addition to taking better care of ourselves, here are more strategies to help manage anger in a healthy way:

- **Identify your triggers:** What situations or people typically make you angry? What do those situations remind you of from your past? Knowing what triggers you is a window into a pain point in your life. Pay attention to that, lean in to it, and let the healing begin.
- **Take a time-out:** When we feel anger rising, taking a few deep breaths and giving ourselves a time-out is gold. Step away from the situation, count to ten, thirty, or a million—just give your brain time to get settled before reacting.
- **Express the underlying emotions:** This is an important one. **It's better to explain how we're feeling than showing it.** Don't bottle up the fact that you're angry; express the fact instead. We can do this calmly and still be assertive: "I feel hurt when . . ." or "I'm feeling frustrated because . . ." is a more productive approach than simply yelling.
- **Practice forgiveness:** Holding on to anger is like drinking poison and expecting the other person to get sick. Forgiveness doesn't mean being okay with someone's behavior; it means letting go of the resentment and anger that's harming you.
- **Seek professional help:** If you're struggling to manage your anger on your own, consider seeking professional help. A therapist can teach you other effective coping mechanisms and help you identify the root causes of your anger.

Remember, anger is a normal emotion; **you most likely don't have an anger problem but just need better ways to respond when you feel overwhelmed.** The goal is to express anger in a healthy way so it doesn't control you. By understanding your triggers, dealing with the emotions underneath, and practicing helpful coping strategies, you can turn that inner volcano into a gentle simmer, allowing you to live with more clarity and calm.

Boogie still walks off leash, and months later there haven't been any hateful comments. The most popular reaction I get is: "She's so well-behaved; my dog could never do that."

ANXIETY FEEDS ANGER, AND ANGER FEEDS ANXIETY.

17.

THOUGHTS

BETRAYING YOURSELF BREEDS ANXIETY

Who am I, what do I like, what do I love, what do I obsess over, how am I difficult to be around, what's my cup of tea, and what's so bitter? For me, even though these questions are important, I often avoid them, because the act of better-defining myself gets scary and makes me feel anxious; it's for those reasons we have to ask them.

Am I a creative, artistic author who dives into the depth of his soul and writes from the darkness he discovers there or just a guy who writes catchy ideas in a digestible way and makes a living by doing it? Should I let go of the stuff that's been successful but feels repetitive and pursue something creative that scares the shit out of me but also lights a fire I rarely feel? Is this passion-driven lifestyle something us humans should even be entitled to? I overthink these questions and spin around, giving myself the illusion that I'm doing something when really I haven't done a thing. Then I realize it's just easier to be who and where I am, because it's safe and comfortable, and anything new is terrifying.

It's clear the masks we wear are suffocating and feed our anxiety, but *we can't be ourselves if we don't know ourselves*. Often we may blame the outside world for robbing us of the chance to be more authentic, but really, it's us strapping on the masks and realizing we'd be lost without it. When we're young, we start climbing a mountain in life, and the idea that we may have chosen the wrong hill is terrifying, but that means we have to climb back down, find a new mountain, and start all over.

These mountains aren't simply career based. Sure I can stop writing books and devote the rest of my life to developing a new art form I call Bearded Ballet,* but what about labels like "mother" or "husband"? These aren't subjective labels we can

* You're welcome for that mental image.

simply throw away and start fresh, like replacing a name tag that reads "Kanwer Singh" with one that reads "Humble the Poet." With that comes a lot of anxiety.

Our identities play an important role in how safe and shameful we feel and how that impacts our mental health, specifically the anxious feelings we have.

None of us enjoy betraying our true selves. **Life has us constantly negotiating between who we really are and who we feel safe to be.** That safety may not be physical but rather emotional and psychological, especially in a world where shame is used as a weapon to keep us in line. Because of this, the way we present ourselves becomes a very careful performance designed to avoid judgment and maintain peace.

We're not weak for needing to put on these performances; it's normal that we treat the thoughts and feelings of others as the mirror through which we view ourselves. That leads us to endlessly chasing approval. What we have to realize, though, is that *this endless chase for validation traps us in a cycle of pleasing people, where our self-worth is always just out of reach, like a carrot on a stick.*

The best way to break this cycle is to define yourself on your own terms. This doesn't mean we have to know exactly who we are right now, but having a sense of direction or a loose idea of who we truly feel we are is better than nothing. Knowing ourselves better helps improve our mental clarity and stability. Remember, anxiety thrives on our lack of focus, so figuring out who we are can act as a guiding beacon through all the decisions we have to make. By understanding who we are—and just as importantly, who we're not—we turn life's complexities into choices that truly align with us.

I struggle with this in dating, my career, and even how I interact with my family. I'm always caught between who I am and who I feel I need to be. Through writing this book, I've realized that "who I feel I need to be" is really "who I feel safe being around others." I only know something is safe because I've experienced it before and nothing bad happened.

For example, what would happen if I shaved my beard? Who would I become? I don't know, and that uncertainty creates a lot of anxiety. It's not really about the beard; it's about my need to control and predict what will happen. That's why we often stick to the status quo instead of trying something new. Life is unpredictable and scary, so we cling to what we know, even though growth comes from stepping into the unknown.

When we spend more time defining who we are at our core, we realize that true **safety doesn't come from seeking approval from others but from minimizing how often we betray ourselves.** Even if we're rewarded for going against our core values, we still have to deal with the negative feelings that come with it. I see this a lot with friends who make a lot of money doing something they hate; they often spend that money to justify the betrayal. In contrast, friends who live in line with their true selves seem to need less and show off less.

When we let our true identity guide us, every decision feels a bit easier, and we feel less lost and overwhelmed. Knowing who we are helps us overthink less and gives us a direction, even if it's not perfectly clear, to move toward.

How do we get to know ourselves?

Self-knowledge and self-awareness involve separating who we truly are from the noise of others' expectations and societal norms, and then organizing what remains.

- Who are we when no one is watching?
- How much of that do we feel safe to show the world?
- What's left, and what does that reveal about us?

I have no desire to shave my beard, but I also don't want to be seen as a self-help guru or social media influencer. Letting go of these labels feels risky because I've worked hard to get here, but what's the point of living behind a mask that doesn't reflect who we truly are?

My therapist told me the reason I seek outside validation is to medicate the fact that I don't exist according to my core values, so I began taking online quizzes to discover who I really am. The biggest thing that stood out to me with that was realizing that I only feel unsafe being myself because the definition of "myself" is a work in progress. I'm making peace with the fact that it's a never-ending process, and, really, my success comes, and my anxiety fades, when I'm aligning with the core values that I'm aware of.*

Let's minimize how often we betray ourselves and see how that relates to how we overthink and have anxious feelings.

* Like my activism work around having mint chocolate chip ice cream banned from the planet.

"WHO I FEEL I NEED TO BE," IS REALLY "WHO I FEEL SAFE BEING AROUND OTHERS."

18.

THOUGHTS

TURNING FOMO TO JOMO

On my lunch break as a teacher, back when Beyoncé was still a Destiny's Child, I stopped by the gas station to grab a coffee.* I remember noticing the hustle and bustle of the station's parking lot—the truck drivers, people pumping gas, a guy buying a lottery ticket—and having a sinking feeling in my chest. I was going to go back into my windowless classroom, and the world was going to keep going on outside.

I was having intense FOMO.

FOMO here is defined as the fear of missing out.

FOMO comes from our basic human need for connection and belonging. We all want to feel included and valued, and when we don't, it triggers a fear of being left out. That feeling of FOMO is like a social pain signal, pushing us to reconnect with others.

At that gas station, there wasn't anything special happening, but the idea that people were going to be outside and I had to be inside made me feel left out.

When we experience FOMO, our brains release stress hormones like cortisol** like it's hosting a 24/7 anxiety marathon, complete with commercials for all your worst fears. Cortisol is meant to help us handle real threats by giving us a boost of energy. But with FOMO, the threat is more in our heads than in real life, so that energy just feels like stress. This constant psychological stress can lead to chronic anxiety, making us feel always on edge and unhappy.

---

* Gas Station Timmies, my Canucks know.

** Chronic stress and high cortisol levels damage the cells responsible for hair pigmentation, so now when I think of cortisol, I think of going gray—or grey, whichever spelling scares you more.

I used a mild example of being at a gas station and feeling jealous that truck drivers get to hit the open road, or that a guy had time to play the lottery in the middle of the day.* But now, our FOMO and the anxiety that comes with it are triggered much more often because of . . . drumroll . . . social media.

FOMO is linked to social comparison, where we measure our worth against others. Social media amplifies this, as everyone presents an edited, highlight-reel version of their life. **The more time we spend on social media, the more likely we are to experience FOMO** and feel anxious about our own lives.

A study from the University of Essex found that people with higher levels of FOMO also spent more time on social media and had increased feelings of stress and anxiety. Ironically, we often check social media to distract ourselves from anxious feelings, not realizing it raises our FOMO, making our anxiety worse.

Living in New York, I could FOMO myself to death. There's always something happening—whether it's a rooftop party, underground art show, or a guy playing spoons on the subway—and I'm pretty sure they're all way cooler than whatever you're doing.

The truth is, I probably am missing out on something magical, but there will always be more. What needs to change isn't my actions, but my mindset. I'm thinking from a place of scarcity when I should be recognizing and embracing abundance.

A friend put it very well: "In New York, say no to 99 percent of the things you're invited to and realize that the 1 percent left is still more fun than anyone else is having anywhere in the world."

Staying home is not a punishment; it's essential to having a fulfilling life. Most of the people wandering the streets in this city are doing it to find someone to come home with them. It still all boils down to connection. And one of the best ways to address the anxious feelings that come with FOMO is to connect with ourselves.

Let's remember that our survival software needs us to focus on what we DON'T have and what's out of place, which is going to worsen our FOMO anxiety, so it's

* He probably needs to hit it big.

up to us to intentionally focus on what we DO have and how wonderful it makes us feel. This is the practice of gratitude.

Modern marketing is designed to make us feel left out if we don't see the latest show, eat at the new restaurant, buy the newest product, or hop on the next viral trend. Understanding our values and knowing what really matters to us helps minimize chasing what everyone else is doing. When we do things that align with our values, there's nothing else to miss out on. Eminem famously skipped the 2003 Oscars, where he won for "Lose Yourself," to watch cartoons with his daughter. That's a man who knows his priorities.

None of us like feeling left out, and FOMO makes it seem like missing something means we don't belong or aren't enough—but you're not getting kicked out of the human race for missing a brunch. It's just an unhelpful thought in a world where there's always something to miss. Even though I'm not a teacher anymore and have the luxury to sit on a beach to write this book,* that FOMO gremlin still whispers anxious thoughts like, "You're still missing out, bro," in my ear.

Following the crowd feels safe, like eating plain toast—it won't hurt you, but is this really living? Going your own way will bring some anxiety, but that's also where the excitement starts. If you're living authentically, shaped by who you are and what you want, there's nothing to miss out on.

Years later, Beyoncé is no longer a Destiny's Child, and I'm no longer working out of a windowless classroom, but I still experience FOMO. Where once I dreamed of the freedom to live wherever and work whenever I want, I now catch myself envying people with more structured lives and jobs they don't have to take home. Our external lives highlight the FOMO, but it's the inner work we do that allows us to be happy where we are, and even experience a little JOMO** every now and then.

* 0% of this book was written on a beach. Honestly, I can't remember the last time I was near a beach—unless scrolling past someone's vacation photos on Instagram counts.

** Joy of missing out.

WE'RE SO BUSY CHASING WHAT WE THINK WE'RE MISSING, WE FORGET TO APPRECIATE WHAT WE ALREADY HAVE.

PART 4:

RETHINKING ANXIETY

19.

THOUGHTS

ANXIETY TELLS US WHAT WE *NEED*, NOT WHO WE *ARE*

I had a short romance with a beautiful soul who would switch to Spanish whenever she couldn't find the right words in English. In the middle of her monologues, she'd say, *"Cómo se dice?"* when she was searching for the right words.

We didn't last very long, but she left a bigger impact than I realized.

A few months later, my friend was on the phone with a food delivery person, trying to explain where the front door of his apartment was. The delivery person spoke no English, and my friend was trying his best to speak Spanish. At one point, I heard him say, *"Cómo se dice?"* and felt a tiny tremor in my body.

Those five syllables brought up a heartbreak I didn't realize I was still experiencing, and that made me sad. Remember, triggers are reminders of past experiences, happy and sad.

After some time, I got a chance to reflect on that experience, the trigger, how it made me feel and think, and what that all meant.

I realized there were three different things: a sensation, a feeling, and an emotion.

A **sensation** is just the basic info our body picks up from the outside world—this relates to our five senses.

A **feeling** is our personal experience, the meaning we give that sensation (excitement and nervousness may give the same sensation, but we call it different feelings).

Emotion is the bigger, more layered response based on what we've been through in the past. It's the full experience, which can include feelings, thoughts, and even actions.

This is important to remember when it comes to anxiety: you're not an anxious person; you're just experiencing anxious feelings at this moment.

Our emotions are echoes of our past, shaping how we see and respond to the world. Sometimes, without us even realizing it, something around us can spark an emotional reaction because it rhymes with a past experience, and we react the same way.

If someone's been through trauma, they might feel anxious in situations that remind them of that time (trigger). Our survival brain is constantly asking, "What does this echo?" when deciding if something poses a threat. This is why new things can feel scary, while old, familiar things that are harmful—like a bad habit or an ex—don't set off any alarms.

Over a decade ago, I was robbed and attacked on the streets late at night. Because my attackers were teenagers, it was difficult for me to comfortably be around crowds of young people for a long time. Anxious feelings would also start when I was alone at night outside.

For others it may be around loud noises; for others it could be riding in a car. These feelings and triggers aren't a reflection of who we ARE, but more about what we've been through.

Our feelings are like those chatty friends who always have something to say. They're not bossing us around; they're more like, "Hey, pay attention to me!" So, when loneliness, shame, or insecurities throw a party in our brain, we don't have to freak out. No need for an identity crisis or future meltdown. Instead, we can greet these feelings with a warm, curious "hello." It's like asking, "What's going on? Why are you stealing the spotlight today?" and "What do you actually need?" It's about exploring our inner world with a little tenderness and a lot of curiosity. You might just discover something new about yourself!

It's important to remember that **our emotions, while giving us clues about our past, don't define who we are.** We're always growing and evolving, and we're more than just our feelings. We're complex, with our own beliefs, values, goals, and dreams. Emotions are temporary—affected by what's going on around us—but they don't decide who we are.

When we identify ourselves by our emotions, it can make us harder on ourselves and stunt our growth. Instead, if we view our emotions as snapshots of the past, we can observe them with curiosity and learn from them rather than judging them.

Feelings are meant to be felt; if you ignore them, they'll just come back stronger, like bad fashion trends.* Allow yourself to feel emotions as they come. Even when it's tough, just breathe with intention while you're doing it. Feelings, especially the anxious ones, are often trying to tell us something.

Even when my survival brain jumps to wild conclusions—like assuming every group of teenagers is a gang of robbers—I've practiced leaning in to those anxious feelings instead of running away. This helps train the brain to understand that just because something triggers a memory of past trauma, it doesn't mean it's a real threat right now.

I had to do this when it came to crowds. I even went back to the exact spot where I was attacked, heart racing, and let myself feel everything. I stood there during the day, giving those anxious feelings room to exist, and eventually they faded. Depending on the trauma, we might need to revisit those "crime scenes" more than once, whether it's physically returning to a place or processing it through journaling or therapy. Giving ourselves space to feel what we need to feel is how we heal.

When I feel stressed or overwhelmed, it's often a sign I need a break or a new perspective. But I won't know that until I acknowledge and express those feelings to see where they lead. It's okay to not be okay—it doesn't mean something's wrong with you. Our emotions are a normal part of being human, and they'll constantly change. They remind us of what we've been through, but they don't define who we are or where we're going.

Let's approach them with curiosity, grace, and kindness, not labels or judgments. **We're not "triggered"—our feelings are.** You're not a sad person; you're a person who feels sad, and that's normal. Creating space between you and your emotions helps you see them for what they really are—temporary states shaped by past experiences.

* Looking at you, high waisted jeans.

> *The emotion you feel is not who you are. It is just a visitor. Welcome it and let it go.*
>
> — **ECKHART TOLLE**

Am I going to avoid all beautiful women who speak Spanish to protect myself from being triggered again? Probably, yes—but for the sake of making a point, I'll lie and say no. These triggered feelings don't define me, but they do highlight where the work still needs to be done. Putting myself in those situations on purpose is a great way to start building resilience, while also letting myself feel everything—not just the pleasant stuff.

So, next time you're out and hear someone say, "*Cómo se dice?*" pause, take a breath, notice where you feel that sensation in your body, and breathe into it. Remind yourself it's okay to feel both happy it happened and sad it's over. Embrace both feelings—they can coexist without defining you.

IT'S OKAY NOT TO FEEL OKAY.

20. THOUGHTS

CHANGE YOUR STORY, CHANGE YOUR ANXIETY

Nine months after moving to New York City, I finally sat down for a meal at a restaurant by myself. It wasn't planned. After dropping Boogie off at the groomer, I had some time to kill. Instead of grabbing a quick slice of pizza, I decided to go to a proper restaurant with a menu. Even though New York is full of people eating solo, the idea freaked me out. Would people stare at me, judge me, think I was weird? Would I get so bored that I'd start folding my napkin into a swan or fake-read my phone like I was getting an urgent email from Taylor Swift?*

I had built up so many stories in my head about eating alone that I avoided it for way too long. And I'm not talking about grabbing something quick at a fast-food spot. I mean sitting down at a full-on restaurant, the kind with unlaminated menus, waiters, and the pressure to chew politely. Even asking the hostess for a "table for one" felt awkward, but she didn't bat an eye. She walked me to my table, took away the extra place setting, and carried on like it was just another Tuesday.

I scanned the room, convinced people were staring at me. And yeah, a few glanced my way, but I couldn't tell if it was because I was solo or just the newest person in the room. The moment someone else walked in, their attention shifted. I nervously googled "tips for eating alone" and saw, "Sit at the bar and chat with the bartender." Cool tip, except the bar wasn't even open yet.

Beside me were two elderly women chatting, and on the other side, a couple of women with a kid enjoying their meal. After a couple of minutes, everything just felt . . . normal. I ordered my broccolini and spaghetti, ate, paid the bill, and left feeling awkwardly proud of myself, like I'd unlocked some secret level of adulthood.

* . . . Or whoever emailed me from shakinitoff@swiftmail.com.

As I walked out, I asked myself, "What would I think if I saw someone eating alone?" And the truth? I've seen plenty of people do it and never gave it a second thought. A few nights earlier, I met a guy at a party who came solo. He admitted the person who invited him wasn't there yet, which ended up being the perfect icebreaker for us to bond over how few people we actually knew in the room.

It's funny how we tell ourselves stories that ramp up our anxiety, when in reality, things aren't nearly as bad as we make them out to be in our head. **The problem isn't our thoughts, it's our thinking.**

We're all storytellers, not just about the world around us but about ourselves too. These stories become our internal scripts, shaping how we see things, how we act, and how much we let anxiety take over. They affect our confidence and often make us give up before we even start. Like I've said before, our brains act like well-meaning bodyguards, trying to protect us from anything they see as a threat. Those bodyguards whisper things like, "This is too hard" or "You're not as smart as . . ." These little statements may seem harmless, but they keep anxious thoughts right at the forefront.

The stories we tell ourselves can easily become self-fulfilling prophecies because obsessing over our pain only makes it grow. When we say something is difficult, it starts to feel even harder, making us more likely to get frustrated or give up. And when we start comparing ourselves, thinking, "I'm not as smart as . . . ," it fuels feelings of inadequacy, stopping us from embracing our own unique strengths.

Here's the good news: our survival brain doesn't have to keep feeding us anxiety-filled stories. We have the power to rewrite the script and become better authors of our own thoughts.

Nina Simone famously said, "Freedom is no fear." When we buy into the negative stories our mind creates, we give our freedom away to fear. But when we choose to focus on our triumphs, we feel more free to move forward.

Try this out: **imagine yourself as the hero of your own story.** Villains see themselves as victims and spread their pain, but heroes see challenges as adventures, failures as stepping stones, and uncertainties as opportunities to grow. This isn't about ignoring the hard stuff or pretending life is always fair—it's about reframing difficulties as chances to build resilience and optimism.

Entrepreneur Alex Harmozi's favorite mantra is ending all his complaints with "and that's okay."

"This is hard . . . and that's okay."

"I'm not as smart as everyone else . . . and that's okay."

"I'm sitting here alone eating broccolini . . . and that's okay."*

Acknowledge the challenges, awkwardness, and discomfort. It's okay to feel anxious and uneasy—those feelings are valid. Just don't let them become the main focus of your story. You get to decide the rest.

Here's how to rewrite your stories for less anxiety:

- **Challenge the negative story:** Don't just believe your anxious thoughts. Ask yourself, "Is this really true? Is this fear talking?" Questioning these thoughts can help break down your anxiety.
- **Flip the "what ifs":** Instead of focusing on bad outcomes, try asking, "What if things go better than I expect?" or "What if people actually like me?" This shift in thinking brings more hope and positivity.
- **Be kind to your anxious voice:** **Instead of fighting anxiety, treat it with kindness.** Imagine it as a scared kid, not a monster. Comfort it, remind yourself of your strengths, and gently steer your thoughts in a better direction.

Remember, the anxious stories we tell ourselves didn't happen overnight. They've been repeated over and over, shaping how we think. Rewriting them will take the same kind of effort—it's a process. Some days, anxiety will still take the spotlight, but as you keep challenging it, you'll grow into a stronger, more confident author of your own life. And that might even inspire others to rewrite their stories too.

My first solo meal was a big milestone. By the time you read this, I'll probably have my own favorite booth at the restaurant, so comfortable eating alone that people will wonder if I'm secretly reviewing the place for *The New York Times*. That's the story I'm telling myself, and I'm sticking to it.

What's the story you need to rewrite today?

* Actually, maybe I'll need a little more practice on this one.

WE HAVE THE POWER TO BECOME BETTER AUTHORS OF OUR THOUGHTS.

21.

THOUGHTS

IT'S IMPORTANT TO BE AN IMPOSTER

What's a real writer? Is it someone who gets paid to write? Someone whose quotes end up on posters with a cheesy sunset backdrop? Maybe it's someone signed to a major publisher or the person drinking overpriced coffee at a café while "working* on their novel" When do we** decide we're real writers and not just imposters pretending?

I thought I'd feel like a real writer when I signed my first book deal or when people started quoting me in elementary schools. But honestly, I didn't feel like a writer until someone asked me to read their manuscript, and I panicked, Googling "how to give polite feedback when it's terrible." That's when I realized that imposter syndrome isn't about what others think of us—it's something we carry inside. And maybe that's not such a bad thing.

We've all had moments where we feel like we don't really belong in our own lives, like we're just pretending to be who we are. That voice in our head says the good things happening are just lucky breaks, and soon enough, we'll get found out as fakes.

That's imposter syndrome.

It's like walking through a funhouse of mirrors, but instead of laughing at the reflections, you start questioning if you even deserve to be there. It makes you feel like you're not the real deal, and everyone else knows what they're doing, while you're just winging it. The truth is, everyone feels this way sometimes—even the smartest, most successful people.

---

* And by "working," I mean watching puppy videos for "research."

** And by "we," I mean "me."

Feeling like an imposter doesn't mean you're not good enough; it just shows you care. The first step is to recognize these feelings and accept them. It's time to stop playing the background and step up as the main character in your own story.

In today's world, no one feels totally qualified. We're constantly told to chase this shifting idea of "enough." Every success can feel like luck, and every time we achieve something, it's easy to feel like a fraud. We stay busy to avoid facing the anxieties that creep up on us.

This hustle culture leads to burnout, which feeds our imposter syndrome even more. We start wondering why we're struggling when everyone else seems to have it together. Those insecurities get louder, drowning out any compliments or validation we get from others.

But here's the thing: the whole idea that you need to be "qualified" to try something new is broken. Life is messy, and we're always figuring it out as we go. Trial and error is how we grow.* **How can you be qualified for something that's never been done before?** Being unqualified means you're pushing boundaries and diving into new territory. We build our wings while falling off the cliff.

You're not an imposter just because you're trying something new—you're a trailblazer. Who's really "qualified" to go to Mars, cure cancer, or invent a floating ice cream cone?** We all fake it until we make it. I wasn't an author until I became one. Hearing my writing hero, John Green, admit he still feels like an imposter after multiple bestsellers and movies really helped me with my own imposter syndrome. Even the pros feel it, and that's okay.

So, how do we handle the anxieties that come with imposter syndrome?

- **Redefine Success:** Forget the idea of fame or fortune. Did you learn something? Did you make it through the day? Congrats, you're already winning. Celebrate every victory, whether it's a big milestone or just the fact that you wore pants today.*** Your journey is the reward.

---

* Fuck around and find out is a great way to live.

** You know, so it just floats beside you and you don't have to hold it and get your hands sticky.

*** Ironically, I'm currently typing this without any pants on . . . I'm wearing shorts, get your mind out of the gutter!

- **Embrace Imperfection**: No one's perfect, and mistakes aren't failures—they're lessons. Instead of seeing slip-ups as proof you're not good enough, treat them as opportunities to grow. A flat tire doesn't mean you should pop the other three. Don't let small bumps turn into giant roadblocks.
- **Silence Your Inner Critic:** You know that voice in your head? The one that's always doubting you? It's time to challenge it. Fight back with self-compassion and kindness. Use affirmations and mindfulness to quiet the negativity.
- **Connect with Others:** You're a human being, not a machine. Disconnect from the noise of social media and focus on real relationships. Imposter syndrome loves isolation, so talk about it with friends, mentors, or a therapist. Sharing your feelings and hearing theirs can help you see you're not alone.
- **Quit Comparing:** We all think everyone else has it together, but spoiler alert: they don't. Everyone's faking it to some degree. Compare yourself only to who you were yesterday, not to other people's highlight reels. You're growing at your own pace, and that's enough.

Self-compassion is the key to dealing with imposter syndrome and all the self-doubt that comes with it. Be as kind to yourself as you would be to a friend. You belong where you are, and what you bring to the table matters. Imposter syndrome will pop up, but that doesn't mean you have to listen to it.

The world pushes us to be productive, not necessarily to feel good about ourselves. So, it's up to us to take control of our happiness. We need to build solid, meaningful connections with our work, creativity, and ourselves. It's okay to slow down, take a breath, and enjoy the journey without constantly chasing some imaginary finish line. Just being here is a win.

You're not alone in feeling like you should be doing more, but "more" is a made-up goal, and chasing it will only burn you out. **There's nothing wrong with you for feeling like something's wrong with you**—that's just human nature. Just being alive and showing up is an accomplishment, even if others don't see it.

And the official definition of a real writer?

Anyone who writes.* Period.

* Bonus points if you occasionally cry over your keyboard for added drama.

FEELING LIKE AN IMPOSTER DOESN'T MEAN YOU'RE NOT GOOD ENOUGH; IT JUST SHOWS YOU CARE.

22.

REACTIONS

WHEN YOUR ANXIETY HAS ANXIETY

It was a late night, back when *Friends* was still teaching us that being "on a break" has lifelong consequences while airing new episodes. I was fueled by caffeine, studying for a coding exam I needed to ace to get into teachers college. As a solid C student, this exam felt like my last chance. Without an A, there would be no degree, no admission to teachers college, no teaching job.*

As I struggled with the material, I suddenly felt a chill. My heart pounded so hard it felt like it would burst out of my chest, and breathing became difficult. I was overwhelmed by a wave of doom and hopelessness, and nothing seemed real. It felt like my life was spiraling out of control, and I was convinced I was going to die right there in that drab study room.

It felt like forever before I could catch my breath and calm myself down, slowly inhaling and exhaling until things returned to normal. I was left sitting there, wiping tears from my eyes, wondering what just happened.

That was my first panic attack, and unfortunately, it wasn't my last.

Panic attacks are like surprise tidal waves crashing into your day, except no one told you they were coming, and you're nowhere near the beach. They can be triggered by certain situations, or they can hit completely out of nowhere, catching us off guard. Luckily, these waves of intense anxiety eventually recede, and we get to feel normal again.

Nervous breakdowns, on the other hand, are like being in rough seas for a long time. Instead of one big wave, it's a prolonged period of choppy waters that make

* Which I'd eventually quit, but you get the stakes.

it hard to think, focus, and handle daily life. This constant turmoil leaves us feeling worn out and overwhelmed, unlike the sharp but brief impact of a panic attack.

Panic attacks strike hard and fast, while nervous breakdowns gradually drain us, making us feel stuck in a never-ending storm. Knowing these differences can help us manage our mental health better and get the right kind of help for each situation.

Once we've experienced an out-of-control episode like a panic attack or nervous breakdown, it's like constantly waiting for a jump scare in a horror movie—except it's our brain pulling all the scares. We're always on edge, bracing for the next wave of anxiety, even when there's no danger in sight.

Triggers for panic attacks and nervous breakdowns can come from both outside and within us. Sometimes it's a buildup of day-to-day stress, and we suddenly hit a limit that causes our survival brain to sound the alarm. Other times, it's dormant trauma that resurfaces at the worst times. Phobias, like spiders, public speaking, clowns, and fresh air,* can also cause panic attacks and nervous breakdowns. Sudden life changes can send us spiraling too.

That's the thing about panic attacks and nervous breakdowns. Our survival brain kicks into overdrive, flooding us with adrenaline and cortisol like we're about to battle a monster. But the "threat" could just be a deadline, low blood sugar—or absolutely nothing at all. With no real threat to fight or run from, that chemical buildup leaves us feeling like an overinflated balloon. Instead of popping, we just float around, full of anxious air, waiting for something to happen.

These episodes are us living in a worst-case scenario that hasn't happened and may never happen. While we can't put ourselves in Bubble Wrap to protect future breakdowns and attacks, there are strategies that can help minimize how often they happen and how intense they feel.

When we choose unhelpful ways to cope, like distractions, avoidance, and medicating the anxiety, then we're only hitting snooze and delaying the inevitable.

The goal is to get more resilient.

The better we eat, sleep, be social, and process the emotions we experience, the more prepared we are to deal with stressful situations.

* Yes—aerophobia is a real thing.

If you find yourself in the middle of a panic attack, just remember **CALM:**

- **C—Chill your breathing:** Take slow, deep breaths. Imagine you're filling a balloon with your belly. Inhale for four seconds, hold for seven, and exhale for eight. This calms your body and mind down.
- **A—Accept what you're feeling:** It's okay to feel panicked. Tell yourself, "This is a panic attack, but it'll pass." Knowing it's temporary can take away some of its power.
- **L—Look around:** Get back to the present moment. Try the 5-4-3-2-1 trick: Find five things you can see, four things you can touch, three things you can hear, two things you can smell, and one thing you can taste. This distracts you from the panic.
- **M—Move or melt:** Do some light stretches, take a walk, or dance like no one's watching* to shake off the tension. You can also try "muscle melting": squeeze different muscle groups for a few seconds, then go loose, starting from your head and working down.

If you find yourself experiencing a nervous breakdown, remember **REST:**

- **R—Recognize the signs:** First, acknowledge that things are tough. It's okay to admit you're feeling stressed or anxious. Understanding what's going on is the first step to feeling better.
- **E—Engage in self-care:** Put yourself first and do things that make you feel good, like taking a long bath, reading a fun book, or listening to your favorite music.
- **S—Seek help:** Don't bottle things up. Reach out to a friend, family member, or therapist. Talking about what's bothering you can help you see things differently and feel less alone. Remember, you've got people who care about you!
- **T—Take a time-out:** Sometimes you just have to say no and step away from the craziness. Take a mental health day, ditch the chores, and give yourself permission to relax. It's okay to hit pause and recharge—in fact, it's essential.

* And if someone's watching, don't break eye contact while you dance.

We're not powerless when it comes to panic attacks and nervous breakdowns. That doesn't mean we can completely rid ourselves of them. I haven't had a panic attack in years, but it may happen again. I enjoy living a life of new experiences and challenges, and sometimes that means ending up in over my head.

A few summers ago, I thought I lost my puppy, Boogie, at the park. The sun went down, and since she's all black, she practically vanished. For a solid 15 seconds, I was spinning around, screaming her name, thinking I'd lost her. Turns out, she was just sitting three feet away, staring at me like I was losing my mind.*

Even though it was a false alarm, the panic was very real. The interesting thing I noticed afterward was my heart rate monitor—it went from 85 to 190** beats per minute very quickly.*** My brain detected a threat, and my body prepared to handle it, even though a racing heart wasn't exactly going to help me find an invisible dog. Still, it was a great lesson in understanding how quickly I get triggered and how my body reacts.

By understanding what triggers us, we can start leaning in to those triggers instead of running away like we're in a cheesy horror movie. Except this time, we get to write the script. Taking care of our mental health is a sign of strength, and by taking charge of our anxiety, we can get back to feeling like ourselves again.

* Her full-time job is to be in my business, why did I assume she'd run away?

** If I drink two cups of coffee and run my fastest on a treadmill, I can barely get up to 180 beats per minute.

PANIC ATTACKS AND NERVOUS BREAKDOWNS ARE LIVING IN A WORST-CASE SCENARIO THAT HASN'T HAPPENED YET AND NEVER WILL.

23.

THOUGHTS

CONTROL FREAKS TO THE FRONT OF THE LINE, PLEASE!

Sometimes life feels like we're spinning a hundred delicate plates all at once. If someone suggested letting one or two crash, we'd probably throw another plate at them for even suggesting such madness. Obviously, if one falls, they'll all fall, so we keep running around, spinning each plate, tending to the ones that demand the most attention while ignoring the ones that seem to be in a good spot for now.

Anxiety often feels like trying to control what can't be controlled. We manage everything—our image on social media, our schedules, our diets—just to feel safe. That's why we want everyone to like us, why we double-check plans, and why we wear workaholism like a badge of honor. As soon as something slips out of our control, our survival brain freaks out and sets off the anxious alarms.

We end up chasing perfection, believing that if we just get everything right, we'll finally feel in control. But when things don't go as planned, we beat ourselves up for not being "perfect," which only makes the anxiety worse.

Control is really tied to fear—fear of not being good enough, making mistakes, or being seen for who we truly are and not being liked. Our survival brain uses fear to protect us from what it thinks is dangerous. But here's the thing: these fears are just part of life, and they're going to happen. In fact, they've probably already happened, and guess what? We didn't die. It's okay to not always feel good enough. Mistakes are normal. And no one is liked by everyone. These fears show our vulnerability, which is actually what makes us real.

I'm not here to tell you to let go of control, because, let's be real—you never had it to begin with. Trying to control life is like herding a bunch of cats for a group photo—it's just not happening. Instead, I want to help you loosen the grip on needing control. Control is an illusion, but it's one that anxiety thrives on. Anxiety is a pro at creating its own illusions, making everything feel like a threat. A time-sensitive email can make your brain react like you're being chased by a velociraptor.*

The illusion of control tricks us into thinking we have more power than we really do. We can't predict how we'll react in new situations, and the fact that we exist on a rock floating in space is a reminder that a lot is beyond our control. Letting go of that need for control can actually ease our anxiety and free us up to live more fully.

Realizing we don't have as much control as we thought shouldn't freak us out—it should help us relax. It takes the pressure off, letting things fall where they may. What happens if we let a few plates fall? They'll crash, maybe make a mess, but life will go on, and you'll realize you probably didn't need that plate anyway.

A lot of our need for control comes from the belief that if we just get over the next hurdle, things will be smooth sailing. But life doesn't work like that. Think about how many times you've promised yourself that your anxiety will disappear once you take care of certain things, only to find that new stressors pop up right after.

I've had my share of existential crises—over money, health, career—where anxiety lingers for years because I had no control over those things. Eventually, I made it through, and while those specific issues don't stress me out anymore, the anxiety still finds new things to latch onto. That's just how it works.

I get anxious about anything that feels uncertain, and uncertainty is basically anything I can't control. The key isn't clinging to control like a cat hanging onto a ledge. It's learning to feel the feelings, even when they're screaming, "What am I doing?" and moving forward anyway. **Overcoming anxiety isn't about getting rid of it—it's about giving it less power by changing how we see it.**

* Fun fact: Raptors were the size of turkeys—thanks for the unnecessary anxiety, Mr. Spielberg.

The moment you accept what you cannot control, you transform the instrument of your torture into a tool of liberation.

— THICH NHAT HANH

But maybe it's not about keeping all the plates spinning.* Maybe the real trick is letting go of the need to control everything. The truth is, not every plate has to stay up. Sometimes letting a few fall** alongside our constant need for control is exactly what we need to find a little more peace in the chaos. Wanting control doesn't mean we're broken, but clinging to the illusion that we can control everything is what's really damaging us.

Surrender isn't about giving up; it's about letting things unfold and choosing curiosity over judgment or guilt. Being a "control freak" won't get you a raise or even a free coffee, but it will add unnecessary stress to your life. Most things are out of our control, and that's actually a good thing. It means there's less for you to worry about, not more.

Ever wonder what Darth Vader, Anxiety, and Control Freaks have in common? Scan the QR code to read the bonus chapter titled: ANOTHER CHAPTER FOR THE CONTROL FREAKS & STAR WARS FANS.

* Who even asked us to join this circus?

** We can always replace them with *paper* plates.

WANTING CONTROL DOESN'T MEAN WE'RE BROKEN, BUT CLINGING TO THE ILLUSION THAT WE CAN CONTROL EVERYTHING IS WHAT'S REALLY DAMAGING US.

24.

ENVIRONMENTS

YOUR COMFORT ZONE CAN COST YOU YOUR RESILIENCE

Think about the last time your Wi-Fi cut out, your phone lost signal, or your battery died. Did you feel frustrated, panicked, or start questioning all your life choices? I get it—losing connection feels like losing a limb. In a world where binge-watching counts as an accomplishment and overnight delivery keeps us glued to the couch, we've wrapped ourselves in a bubble of convenience. The problem with that bubble is the more comfortable we get, the worse we handle life's inevitable challenges—and that's exactly where anxiety loves to throw a party.

We're freaking out over small disruptions—not just when the Wi-Fi's down, but anytime something we rely on disappears. Back in the days of rotary phones, rabbit ear antennas, and waiting two weeks for mail-order CDs, resilience wasn't a luxury; it was a survival skill. If your Walkman batteries died, you just . . . walked and listened to your own thoughts. And no, nobody delivered pizza at the push of a button. You either called or just ate cereal. But with all these modern comforts, we're losing what makes us tough—and the less tough we are, the more anxiety we feel.

Even though we're constantly making life safer—especially those of us lucky enough to be far from major conflicts—we're more sensitive to perceived threats. Our internal alarm system goes off more often, anxieties shoot higher, and we react to imagined dangers more frequently.

This is because we're in what neuroscientist Alex Korb calls a "**challenge deficit.**" Our survival brains are always on edge, trying to detect the next danger, and when it doesn't find it, it assumes it's hiding under the bed. This leaves us in a state of paranoia and unease, making us feel triggered by almost anything new and unfamiliar.

We're building a world without challenges, but it's the challenges that make us stronger. They're like sandpaper for our anxious minds—rough, uncomfortable, but necessary to smooth out the jagged edges of our fears. **Without challenges, we become emotional marshmallows, melting in the convenience microwave.**

We're designed to get stronger from facing a hard world, but instead, we're becoming fragile by living in an easy one. That's why we need to take our resilience into our own hands. Challenges and discomfort are what build inner strength and self-respect.

Studies show that regular exposure to controlled stress—like cold showers or public speaking—can rewire our nervous system, making us less reactive to the things that normally trigger anxiety. Even small steps outside our comfort zones can activate these positive effects.

Here are a few practical steps:

- **Embrace mindful discomfort:** Push yourself to face small, controlled challenges. Try a cold shower, take a hike without your phone, or tackle a tough conversation instead of avoiding it. Start small, celebrate the little wins, and watch your tolerance for discomfort grow. I end every shower with cold water—it sucks every time, but I'm proud of it, and, hey, I'm still here.
- **Relearn the art of effort:** Pick activities that require real mental or physical effort. Spend a weekend tech-free, cook from scratch, or learn a new skill. Overcoming these challenges builds confidence and resilience. When you hit a wall, don't look for distractions. Take a breath, slow down, and keep going—you'll be amazed at how far you can get.
- **Seek out real-world experiences:** Break out of your comfort bubble by volunteering, joining a club, or striking up a conversation with strangers. Social connections help ease anxiety by reminding us we're not alone on this big, spinning rock.

- **Reframe your perspective:** See challenges as invitations for growth, not threats. "What doesn't kill you makes you stronger" isn't just a cliché—it's a resilience mantra. Every obstacle you overcome adds to your inner strength and self-respect. And if it does kill you, well, you're dead, so who cares?

Remember, stepping out of your comfort zone isn't really optional. Sure, it feels safe, but life has a way of yanking us out of it when we least expect it. By challenging ourselves outside of it on purpose, we build the resilience we need for those tough times. Comfort zones only become the enemy to our growth when we try to make them our permanent home. It's better to see them as temporary rest stops—a place to regroup, recharge, and then get back out there to tackle the challenges ahead.

Resilience isn't about being tough to show off; it's about enjoying life with less anxiety. *Go looking for discomfort before it finds you.* As Rumi (probably) said, "The wound is the place where the light enters you." It's through our cracks and vulnerabilities that we grow and gain the strength to handle life's storms.

I love modern conveniences, but they come at a price: our ability to handle unfamiliar situations without extra anxiety. In a world that sells us bigger, faster, brighter, newer solutions to inconveniences we didn't know we had, there's value in choosing the hard way. It's the cost of getting stronger, being more resilient, and spending less time feeling anxious.

Next time the Wi-Fi goes out, or your phone battery dies, don't huff and puff. Smile, take a breath, and make the best of the situation, because you already practiced spending time away from these things. Maybe there's a nice book written by a semi-handsome beardo around that you can enjoy.*

* Feel free to DM me and say I'm fully handsome. I'm totally fishing for compliments.

WE'RE BUILT TO GROW STRONGER IN A TOUGH WORLD, BUT WE'RE BECOMING WEAKER BY LIVING IN ONE THAT'S TOO EASY.

25.

REACTIONS

OUR EMOTIONAL SEESAW CAN TURN OUR HIGHS TO LOWS

When Facebook first kicked off in the mid-2000s, I did what everyone did—I searched my name, Kanwer. Not out of vanity, of course, but just to make sure there weren't any other Kanwers out there stealing my thunder. I found a KanwAr Singh—a.k.a. Sikh Knowledge—out in Montreal, who also rocked a turban and made music. Aside from the unforgivable crime of spelling his name with an *A* instead of an *E,** we hit it off. Turns out, we shared more than just a name—our birthdays were only a day apart. I was July 12,** and he was July 13, and since I was born at 11:45 P.M., I like to think we're basically twins . . . just separated by 15 minutes and questionable spelling choices.***

We made music together, with our biggest hit being a song titled "Baagi Music."**** While the world knew us as Humble & Sikh, we were KanwEr and KanwAr. Sikh eventually moved to Toronto, and our friendship grew; with that, our productivity and collaboration dwindled. One random night in July, Sikh called me up and said, "Hey, I know it's last minute, but let's throw a joint birthday party." Naturally, because what's better than last-minute chaos?

Within a week, we found a spot, invited people, and got a whole birthday party set up. Shockingly, a ton of people showed up—like, way more than I thought. It wasn't a fancy Kardashian-level soirée; it was more like friends, family, and exes.***** With

* Spelling Punjabi names in English always leads to horrific results.

** Save it in your calendar.

*** Also, he's left-handed, but we accept him despite that.

**** It's still on streaming services.

***** Yes, they showed up too.

well over 100 people there, and Sikh mistakenly eating a whole bag of weed cookies and DJing an amazing set, it was a perfect night.

Then came the morning after.

No hangover, no surprise money requests for club damage, and no one mysteriously losing a glass slipper. But there was something worse—me, feeling like I'd just been dumped by the universe. How could I go from having one of the best nights of my life with the people I care about to feeling trapped in a dark hole of melancholy, existential dread, and anxiety?

I've heard friends talk about this too. After winning awards, having amazing life milestones, or having a great night out, the next day feels like a reality check from the universe, a huge feeling of dread, mixed with the reminder that we left our wet laundry in the wash overnight and forgot to put it in the dryer.

Recently, I had an amazing date that went well into the night with someone I had a massive crush on, only to have her end things with me a few days later. She shared that the night was amazing for her, but that the next morning she woke up super depressed and took that as a sign that we shouldn't move forward.

You've probably felt that urge to bail when something seems *too* good to be true. It's not because something's wrong with us; it's just our survival brain sensing an imbalance and sounding the alarm.

There's a concept called *opponent process theory*, by psychologist Richard Solomon, that explains this. It says every emotion has a counter emotion to keep things balanced. So, when you're on a high, your brain's like, "Okay, don't get too cozy, here comes the low to even things out." Emotions are like a seesaw—when you feel something really positive, there's a negative feeling lurking in the background. So, when joy fades, the brain swings back, moving you from the high to the low to keep the balance.

This isn't about our brains trying to ruin our happiness; it's more about keeping us balanced. **When we feel intense excitement or joy, our survival brain thinks it's doing us a favor by releasing some negative emotions to bring us back to neutral.** At first, that negative feeling hides in the background, but as the excitement fades, it creeps in—sometimes taking us even lower than where we started.

I get it, staying in a constant state of excitement isn't practical, so I appreciate my brain trying to keep me calm. But instead of just gently tapping the brakes, it can slam on the brakes hard, and that sucks, especially when we don't know why it's happening.

We start questioning everything: "Was I imagining it? Did people actually have fun? Will this be the last fun thing I ever do?" And in trying to make sense of those negative feelings, we end up making them worse.

Dr. Solomon's theory is just that—a theory. It doesn't mean every good thing will be followed by something bad, but it does give us insight into why those high highs sometimes lead to low lows. It's not that we're broken; our brains just balance out intense emotions in ways that aren't always pleasant. The issue is, our brain doesn't give us a heads-up, so we're left wondering why we suddenly feel off.

Knowing this helps us ride the emotional waves—kind of like understanding that a night of tequila shots leads to the inevitable next-morning "Why am I like this?" If I had known about opponent process theory back then, I would've given myself more grace to deal with the post-party blues, like how we rest after an intense workout.

As we live for those core memories, being aware of this balancing act helps us budget for the emotional aftermath. It's okay to savor the highs, even if negative feelings creep up afterward. **Feeling low after a good time doesn't mean you're bad at happiness or ungrateful.** It's just your survival brain doing its dramatic thing, like, "Oh, you're happy? Cool, here's an existential crisis to keep you grounded." It's a normal part of being human, like having snot in our nose or a single hair on our nipple.* It may not be ideal, but it's the existence we get.

We did throw another birthday party a few years later, but since I left Toronto, my birthday celebrations have been as exciting as watching paint dry. But now, I think I'm ready to hop back on the emotional rollercoaster and plan another epic night—hopefully with fewer regrets and no mystery bruises this time.**

* I've said too much.

** I've said too much again.

FEELING LOW AFTER A GOOD TIME DOESN'T MEAN YOU'RE BAD AT HAPPINESS OR UNGRATEFUL—IT'S JUST PART OF BEING HUMAN.

HUMBLE THE POET

26.

THOUGHTS / HABITS

ANXIETY & CONFIDENCE WON'T HOLD HANDS

Kids can be jerks, it's a part of being a kid.* Empathy develops slowly and doesn't even start to fully take shape until around the age of eight. Combine that with growing up in emotionally and physically unsafe homes, and some children won't develop much empathy at all.

I have to remember this when I relive my stories of being targeted by bullies. Being a little kid with a top knot of hair on his head, I was picked on regularly. I didn't always have long hair—I used to be a mushroom-cut kid like everyone else back in the 80s—and it wasn't until the third grade when I wore a small patka** to class that I instantly felt like I didn't belong. I was picked on endlessly, called names, stared at, pointed at, and even attacked, just for looking different. By the age of 10, I was already dreading those taunting words and cruel sneers whenever I entered an unfamiliar space. These encounters were anything from people endlessly staring, to outright racist remarks, to acts of violence, from kids and adults alike.

I didn't realize how much those moments impacted me until I got older and took the time to reflect. There's scar tissue from those experiences that I still carry today, especially when I walk into new spaces. When I make eye contact with an attractive stranger, my first thought is often that they see me as gross or "the other." Even though I have countless experiences that prove otherwise, the cringe and negative assumptions still sneak in.***

* Fun fact: 100 percent of adults who are jerks were once kids.

** A head covering wrap for my top knot of hair.

*** I'm not fishing for any compliments here, but if you want to send me some, don't hold back ;).

Sometimes my assumptions aren't that far off. I once dated a girl who told me her mom thought I was handsome but wanted me to shave my beard—a beard that's both culturally and spiritually important to me. How people, especially those we care about, see us can really mess with how we feel about ourselves.

This kind of stuff eats at my confidence and holds me back. I constantly talk myself out of things. When I first started posting online as Humble the Poet, I refused to show my face. The truth I was avoiding—and still sometimes ignore—is that I actually have no clue what people think or feel when they see me. My assumptions are just me trying to read their minds, but in reality, it's all about how I feel about myself. Whatever they think of me often tells more about them than about me.

This is true for all of us—it's woven into our stories. The way we see ourselves shapes our world, influencing the paths we take and the doors we choose to open or close. When we look at life through the filter of our self-worth and confidence (or lack of it), it impacts our anxiety, shaping not just how we handle stress, but also how we face opportunities and challenges.

How we view ourselves also affects how we interact with and make sense of the world around us.

Robert Kleck at Dartmouth University conducted a study known as "The Dartmouth Scar Experiment." In this experiment, he took people who were applying for jobs and gave them a noticeable, fake scar on their face. He told them it was for a different study. Before their actual job interview, half of the participants were told the fake scar was removed, while the rest believed they still had it on. The truth was that *all* of them had their scars removed.

The results: the people who thought they still had a scar performed less confidently than the people who believed they didn't. Some even reported that the interviewer for the job was rude, unkind, and stared at their "scar."

This experiment shows how the way we see ourselves—our internal scars—decide our success and interactions on the outside.

Our self-worth is our ceiling. We subconsciously limit our potential, success, and happiness to match what we believe we deserve. This invisible ceiling touches every area of our lives—how much we earn, the relationships we settle for, and even the choices we make, like what we buy or where we shop.

The way we see ourselves affects how others see us too. People pick up on the signals we send and will treat us the way we treat ourselves. If we doubt our worth, others will follow suit. If we fear rejection, we'll hold back and stay in unhealthy relationships. When we don't practice self-love, we might turn to emotional eating, substance abuse, or neglect our health, believing on some level that this is all we deserve.

The good news? Our self-worth isn't set in stone—it can grow. To improve the quality of our lives, we have to start with the relationship we have with ourselves.

This involves:

- **Celebrating yourself:** Think of how Apple hypes up every product like it's revolutionary, even if something similar already exists. Do the same for yourself. Stand in front of the mirror and give yourself genuine compliments with that same level of excitement.
- **Choosing a part of yourself that you love:** Even if you're not feeling great about your body overall, find at least one part you do like. Maybe it's your eyes, your smile, or even something quirky like your crooked nose or a patchy beard. Focus on that feature and appreciate it for what makes it unique.
- **Spotting the bad stuff:** Pay attention to the things or people that bring out self-doubt or make you feel less than. These triggers highlight areas to work on and can help you understand why certain things affect your self-worth.
- **Facing what scares you**: Don't avoid what brings fear or sadness. Confronting these emotions, rather than running from them, is an essential step toward building a stronger, more confident version of yourself.
- **Building a better view of yourself:** Speak kindly to yourself. Positive self-talk can help you shift how you see yourself and gradually improve your self-worth.

The anxious voices feeding your insecurities aren't the enemy—they're misguided friends trying to keep you safe. Their goal is to protect you by keeping you in your comfort zone, but that only shrinks your world and holds you back from living fully. You're more valuable and worthy than you realize. Those voices that tell you otherwise are just scared. The hurtful people from your past may have left scars, but those scars aren't permanent—they're like temporary tattoos you can wash away.

As for me, it's been a journey of baby steps—talking to more strangers, taking leaps without knowing where I'll land, and feeling the fear but doing it anyway. My turban's gotten taller, my beard's gotten longer, and I always give the guy in the mirror a wink and a smile. Embracing and celebrating myself, while also discovering my insecurities, will be a lifelong process—and I'm good with that. I'm excited to see how far you'll take your own journey.

To love oneself is the beginning of a lifelong romance.

— OSCAR WILDE

PEOPLE TREAT YOU THE WAY YOU TREAT YOURSELF. IF YOU DOUBT YOUR VALUE, OTHERS WILL TOO.

HUMBLE THE POET

PART 5:

DEALING WITH THE ANXIETY OF OTHERS

27.

REACTIONS

ANXIETY WARPS OUR LOVE LIVES

In moments of intense anxiety, all I want is to FaceTime someone, lay my head in their virtual lap, have them play with my beard through the screen, and gently tell me, "Hey, you're not a piece of trash, and everything will be fine." But instead, I get Siri reading back my grocery list.* Or I end up calling someone who's also looking for that same comfort, and now we're two anxious babies, desperate for reassurance and frustrated and resentful that neither of us can provide it.

We're often told to follow our heart, as if it's a magical compass that will lead us to everything we need. But when we're anxious and overthinking, that compass spins wildly. Instead of looking for real love and connection, we chase anything that eases our feelings of inadequacy.

We start to see relief from anxiety as love. **We think love will fix us, but the truth is, we're not broken.** The real issue is our struggle with self-worth.

The idea of a relationship is exciting because it feels like a safe space that will magically heal our feelings of not being good enough. This might work for a while, but it fades quickly. **Relationships reveal our wounds, they don't heal them.** They just hold up giant mirrors and yell, "See? Still There!" Understanding this is the first step to realizing why, especially during anxious overthinking, we crave connections that don't actually help us build genuine self-worth.

Our problems with self-esteem, self-worth, and self-respect start from inside. No one else can truly fix them. Sure, getting attention or praise might feel good for a while, but it's like a bandage that eventually falls off.

* Remind me to get milk.

Relationships can help us understand ourselves better. They're not a magic cure for all the hurts, but they can be amazing X-ray machines that show us what's really going on inside. I don't like the idea of "love languages," but they're easy to understand. We can use them to see how our flaws might show up in our relationships.

- **Acts of service:** People who value acts of service often have trouble asking for help, which shows a struggle with vulnerability.
- **Quality time:** Wanting quality time but fearing real intimacy can lead to distancing ourselves from our partner.
- **Physical touch:** We might love physical touch but avoid it as a way to protect ourselves from the perceived threat of closeness.
- **Gift giving:** Gift giving can be linked to impulsive shopping, suggesting a search for fulfillment through things rather than emotional connection.
- **Words of affirmation:** In craving words of affirmation, we might go quiet, silently seeking attention and validation.
- **Snacking together:** I made this one up to show how easy it is to create love languages.

Our anxiety in relationships can tell us a lot about ourselves. For example, I'm afraid of "settling" in love. This fear comes from feeling insecure and not good enough. It's like I'm trying to protect myself by not getting too close.

I used to feel like I was settling with my job as a teacher. But when I became an artist, I felt more excited and alive. I promised myself I would never settle again, even in my love life. The problem is, I started focusing more on finding something new than on building strong relationships and deep connections.

We're all looking for someone who's interesting, but the problem is we often chase what's exciting rather than what we can genuinely connect with. This search for emotional entertainment never ends. It can become an addiction, constantly seeking the thrill of new experiences and mistaking that for real connection. This cycle, driven by a fear of being stuck, pulls us away from the depth and authenticity we truly want. That's why we need to be careful about looking for a "spark."

The spark isn't real.

The spark is just a triggered emotion, like clickbait for the heart. It grabs our attention but doesn't keep us engaged. Instead of looking for a spark, focus on creating real connections and striking the match yourself, and maybe bring some marshmallows for the inevitable bonfire of emotions.

We sometimes put our partners on a pedestal, thinking they can fix our problems. This creates an unhealthy balance, where we see them as better than us, almost like a parent figure, and rely on their approval for our self-worth. When we don't get enough approval, we spiral into anxiety and overthinking. This way of seeing love not only disrupts balance in relationships but also traps us in a cycle of seeking validation from those we view as better than us.

We must remember that everyone's human, with their own quirks, flaws, and funny smells. Just like us, they're on a journey of growth, making mistakes along the way. The hierarchy in love is an illusion. To foster healthier, balanced relationships, we need to see ourselves as equals, deserving of love and respect.

I've had to learn to stop viewing the women in my life as princesses high up in towers. They don't need my worship or saving. They're people, just like me.* We're both amazing, and we both suck. Being in a relationship means deciding to be amazing and sucky together.

The closest thing to a magic pill in love and anxiety is communication.

Clear communication is what paves the path to healthy relationships. My therapist bluntly told me that my non-negotiable for a partner is someone who's a world-class communicator.** Expressing yourself can help reduce anxiety. It's important to be with someone who values open communication. Talking about your thoughts and feelings can create a stronger bond and help you stop overthinking.

When we're anxious, we might look for quick fixes, even if they're not the best. This can stop us from building meaningful relationships. We*** are constantly chasing the next shiny thing, hoping it'll heal us, but that's not what relationships exist for. Relationships can only show us the wounds, not heal them; that's our job.

A friend was telling me about his struggles with his new girlfriend. He described the issue and explained the unique quirk in her personality, but then maturely said, "And that's something I'm going to have to grow and learn to work with." He

* They just have better skin care routines, and strange desires to cover the bed with millions of pillows.

** It's good advice that I ignore often.

*** And by we, I mean ME.

understands that *relationships are vehicles for our growth, not a parking spot for our insecurities*; that's something we'd all* benefit from remembering.

Let's take people off pedestals, express ourselves more, and use our interactions to learn about and evolve ourselves. Realize that our heart compass will only stop spinning when we slow down, take a breath, and focus on finding love within ourselves, not just chasing it around us.

> *Falling in love won't fix your life, healing your emotional history will.*
>
> — **YUNG PUEBLO**

If you want to explore the anxiety related to your attachment and dating styles, scan the QR code to read the bonus chapter: DATING DRAMA & ANXIETY.

* Including me.

RELATIONSHIPS REVEAL OUR WOUNDS, THEY DON'T HEAL THEM.

HUMBLE THE POET

28.

REACTIONS

THERE'S NO SUCH THING AS BEING TOO NEEDY

I have all these memories of trying to share something with my family and feeling completely shut down. This was anything from sharing good news, bad news, or just recommending a movie. You know when you post a meme in the group chat, expecting at least one "lol," but instead you get crickets? That's what my family interactions felt like—except there were no crickets. Just . . . nothing.

I quickly realized those shutdowns weren't them telling me to shut up; it's more like they didn't even realize I said something. It didn't have to be heavy or deep. It could be simply sharing what happened in the day or asking them to leave something on when they were flipping through channels, only to be ignored.

As a kid, you learn quickly to stop expressing your needs when that happens. What's the point, right? As adults, that strategy sticks. When our needs aren't met, instead of expressing them, we grow passive-aggressive or resentful, just wishing someone could read our mind and give us what we want, even if we don't even know what we need.

Add in social media psychologists who'll say anything for likes,* and suddenly, we're blaming your bad mood on Mercury being in Gatorade. We start to romanticize putting others first, calling ourselves "selfless givers," when really, it's just a lack of self-care. We're not doing anyone any favors by neglecting our own needs.

We feel like we're too much, too needy, too sensitive. We don't want to seem clingy, desperately seeking affection. So instead, we bury what we need and cope with distractions, thinking it's better than saying what we want and not getting it. Here's something to consider: *there's no such thing as being "too needy" or "too*

* Devil bless these horrific algorithms.

sensitive." Feeling these things is no different from feeling hungry when we don't get enough food.

Needing love and connection isn't being needy; it's being human. Just like we need air, water, and a box of cookies in the middle of the night, our brains are wired to crave emotional nourishment; it's a survival thing. When we're low on emotional connections, we have anxious feelings, and our inner alarm goes nuts, screaming, "Feed me!"

That deep craving for connection, for someone to truly see us and fill the emptiness inside, isn't something to dismiss with "stop being so needy." This craving isn't a flaw; it's a signal we need to pay attention to. We're like wanderers in an emotional desert, desperate for a drop of affection. It's not about being too needy; it's about being deprived for too long.

This desperation leads us to text constantly, looking for reassurance. Our insecurities flare up, and we think silence or delayed replies mean rejection. We might even become controlling, trying to hold on tightly to the love we crave, forgetting that love, like water, flows best when it's free.

I think maybe it's all about
not wanting to be alone.
Not wanting to be forgotten.
Not wanting to be left behind.

— CHUCK PALAHNIUK

Loneliness isn't a lack of people; it's a lack of connection, with others and with ourselves. I know this feeling firsthand, living in one of the most crowded cities on earth and still feeling alone at times. Even at parties or gatherings, I can feel isolated if I'm not connecting with anyone. My fear of bothering the people I feel close to stops me from calling them, but I rarely think that maybe they feel the same way, and a call might be exactly what they need.

The way to address loneliness isn't by drowning in our desperation or hiding it behind indifference. It's about nurturing that emptiness inside with self-love and understanding. It's about dealing with our need for connection not through temporary outside validation but with things that truly satisfy us, like self-compassion, healthy boundaries, and meaningful relationships.

Self-compassion is like growing a garden in that desert. The seeds that need watering are our mindfulness and awareness of our emotional needs and triggers. The activities that bring us joy are like plant food. The fences around the garden are our healthy boundaries, protecting us from emotional manipulation and unhealthy situations.

Even with a flourishing garden, we'll still crave connection with others. But now, from a place of strength and self-worth, we can seek out healthier people and show up as our true selves. Remember, you can't be yourself if you don't know yourself. We can open up to genuine friendships, where support matters more than competition. We can build relationships based on mutual respect and shared vulnerability, not desperate dependence.

The more we build genuine connections, the less anxious and needy we'll feel. It's like creating an oasis in that emotional desert. The more love we receive and the stronger our relationships become, the less desperate we'll feel. When our needs are met, we feel more secure and less anxious, and we become more eager to share what we have instead of just looking for what we lack.

Therapist and researcher Dr. Sue Johnson* tells us we're built for "attachment resonance." Our brains light up when we feel seen, heard, and cared for by loved ones. Oxytocin, the "love hormone," floods our system, reducing stress and boosting our well-being. This isn't some abstract idea; it's part of our hardwired biology.

Remember, **needing connection doesn't make you a burden. It's not just up to others to bring connection your way.** Building strong connections requires all of us to be more intentional, vulnerable, open, and trusting. We need to understand that the anxious feelings we have when we crave more connection are just signals of what we're missing.

* Not to be confused with Canada's favorite sex educator, Dr. Sue Johanson.

It's tough when our needs aren't met, especially in childhood, but we can change the story. The new story empowers us to take charge of our emotional well-being by making healthy choices to meet those needs.

My family isn't a bunch of bad people; they're regular, wonderful people who, like many of us, sometimes get caught up in their own thoughts. There's no point in resenting them for being imperfect or unable to meet all my emotional needs. As an adult, I can take care of myself, seek out the connections I want, and put effort into the great relationships I already have.

YOU'RE NOT TOO SENSITIVE OR TOO NEEDY. YOU'RE HUMAN, WIRED FOR EMOTIONAL CONNECTION.

29.

HABITS

SEEKING REASSURANCE IS A TRAP!

I got food poisoning recently. How, you ask? Probably from the roulette wheel of bad choices I made at fast-food joints that day. I'm guessing it was the chicken sandwich that had a secret life as sushi. No matter the culprit, the "double whammy"* hit hard. I spent the night forming a deep, emotional connection with the toilet—bonding over a "both ends" experience. Between rounds, I sipped water like it was some life-saving elixir, convinced I was one dehydration spell away from becoming a cautionary tale on WebMD.

Dehydration is real, but would I actually *die* after this one-two punch of digestive disaster? Google assured me I would. Yes, I googled my symptoms and immediately went into the rabbit hole of all the horrific potentials of my condition.** When I wasn't throwing up, I was researching which foods wouldn't finish me off. Living in the United States without health care,*** I desperately needed reassurance that I wasn't going to die.

The problem wasn't just that I googled my symptoms once; it was that I became a full-time reassurance addict. I'd refresh the same search results like they were stock prices, hoping to finally see, "You're fine, stop being dramatic." But instead of calming my anxiety, each search cranked it up a notch, making me feel even more frantic and out of control.

* Don't google it.

** Google never exaggerates, right?

*** That's a whole other conversation.

My survival brain saw my bathroom party and went straight into panic mode, flooding me with thoughts of doom. To snooze those alarms, I did what we all do—I jumped online, desperately searching for answers and trying to predict how long this misery would last.

When we feel anxious, our gut reaction is to calm it down, usually by seeking reassurance. At first, it feels like a quick fix—whether it's kind words from friends or some WebMD scrolling to guide us through the fog of uncertainty. But what happens when that search for comfort turns into a maze? Instead of easing the anxiety, it can trap us in our own minds, making the anxious feelings worse.

Seeking reassurance starts innocently enough—like sending a text meant for your best friend to your boss instead. Suddenly your stomach's in knots, your face is flushed, and you're mentally preparing to hand in your resignation over a clever, but very inappropriate, combination of emojis. You have a right to feel anxious and worried. The thought of your boss seeing something personal or out of context sends your heart racing and your mind spinning with worst-case scenarios.

You feel a wave of panic and start texting your friends for reassurance, hoping they'll say, "It's no big deal," or "They won't even notice!" But even after you get that reassurance, the anxiety often lingers. The truth is, **chasing reassurance is like drinking salt water when you're thirsty**—it might feel good at first, but it only makes you thirstier.

Instead of calmly asking, "What's happening?" it's more like, "What terrible thing from my past does this vaguely remind me of, so I can freak out properly?" When we get reassurance—like someone reminding us that we sent a similar text before and everything was fine—it does make us feel better for a minute. But the issue is that our survival brain gets used to relying on that reassurance to calm down, and soon it's asking for it all the time.

Every time we seek reassurance, we chip away at our ability to handle anxious feelings on our own. This weakens our resilience, making us more sensitive to anxiety in the long run.

Now, food poisoning might not be your go-to anxiety trigger. Maybe it's checking your bank account every 15 minutes just to confirm you're still broke, or sending four texts in a row because someone hasn't replied in 18 seconds, and obviously, they hate you now. It could be asking your sister to double-check your book for spelling mistakes* when really you just want to know if it's garbage. Or maybe it's as simple as re-opening your phone 25 seconds after posting a picture to see if the digital love likes and hugs are rolling in yet.

Whatever your flavor of anxiety, the chase for reassurance can look different, but it's the same game.

The real damage from the reassurance trap? It's not just asking for reassurance—it's becoming a reassurance junkie.** Suddenly you're hooked on outside validation,*** needing it to calm down. That addiction shapes how we interact with others and makes us more vulnerable when we can't get that quick fix. When we can't be soothed right away, new worries pop up, and we end up with even more anxiety, spiraling further out of control. It's a vicious cycle that chips away at our ability to self-soothe and trust ourselves.

Then *seeking reassurance becomes a temporary cure that leads to long-term sickness.* The more we depend on it, the more we lose the ability to manage anxiety on our own. It turns into both comfort and a crutch.

I realized I'd fallen deep into the reassurance trap when I lost cell service in the elevator and panicked because I couldn't google whether my banana was about to be my stomach's best friend or its worst enemy.

So how do we wiggle our way out of this reassurance trap?

- **Acknowledge the trap:** Recognizing the cycle is the first step. Understand that seeking constant reassurance, as tempting as it is, weakens our resilience and strengthens anxious feelings.
- **Challenge the thoughts:** We don't have to trust everything we think. Ask yourself: "Is this thought helpful?" and "Is this based on evidence or fear?"

* Despite working with the world's greatest editor.

** Side effects include overthinking, excessive googling, and convincing yourself your dog secretly judges you.

*** Like it's the last box of Thin Mints during Girl Scout cookie season.

- **Developing coping skills:** There are endless ways to address anxious thoughts and learn to manage them.
- **Practice self-reliance:** The goal isn't for things to be easier; the goal is to be stronger so you have the resilience to work through the hard stuff. The more we can depend on ourselves, the less power anxiety will have over us. I had to remind myself that I've been much sicker than this and with time this too would get better and how rarely the worst-case scenario* happens.

Instead of worrying if I'm constantly making the wrong decisions and seeking assurance and validation from others, I need to own the idea that sometimes I'll get it wrong and remind myself that I'll be strong enough to deal with it.

My friend Ed Mylett said something that really stuck with me: "What if all the directions are the right way?" That simple idea inspired me to seek out the gems in whatever choices I make, no matter how things turn out.

It's okay if I eat the wrong food and get sick again. That exposure to discomfort helps retrain my brain to find safety within myself rather than external validation.

We're all experiencing the consequences of the reassurance trap and the anxiety that comes with it. The moment we recognize that we're in it is the moment we're one step closer to breaking free from it. By shifting our reliance from outside sources of comfort to our inner strength, we not only grow our resilience but also feel more empowered to expand our lives beyond the limitations we set to avoid facing our anxiety.

Now, when I feel a tiny bit triggered every time I walk by a fast-food spot, that's a great example of anxiety working to ensure I don't make this mistake again. We often forget **anxiety is here to protect us,** and when it's working correctly,** it's like our own personal bodyguard. Goodbye, sketchy chicken sandwiches; hello, $20 salads with organic lettuce and a side of dignity.

* Vomiting until I turn inside out.

** It works correctly as often as your phone autocorrects to the word you actually ducking meant.

CONSTANTLY CHASING REASSURANCE IS LIKE DRINKING SALT WATER WHEN YOU'RE THIRSTY.

30.

THOUGHTS

WHEN YOU ASSUME, YOU MAKE AN ANXIOUS ASS OUT OF U & ME

Imagine this: I'm at a concert in Brooklyn, feeling a bit uneasy because I sense someone staring at me. I glance over and see a guy with red hair, holding a beer and staring at me like he's trying to figure something out. *Maybe he's just drunk*, I think. I try to ignore him, but he gets closer, and I start to tense up. My friend had gone to the bathroom, leaving me alone.

My anxiety skyrockets. I slip my hands into my pockets, wrapping my keys between my fingers like makeshift brass knuckles. "Is this guy trying to start something?" I wonder. Flashbacks of being picked on by a little racist redheaded menace in elementary school flood my mind. I'm triggered, high alert mode activated, like I'm about to face off with a ginger-villain in a low-budget action movie, and I don't have a stunt double.

Then he's right beside me.

"Are you Punjabi?" he asks, smiling.

Caught off guard, I step back and reply, "Yeah."

His eyes light up. "Oh my god, I just got back from Chandigarh. I spent four months there living with a family. I've been so depressed and missing them. I came to the concert to cheer myself up, and seeing you makes me feel like I found a piece of home here."

My shoulders drop. Out of all the wild scenarios I imagined for why this guy was staring—everything from serial killer in training to cult recruiter—seeing me as a piece of "home" wasn't even on the radar.

I was acting like a mind reader, assuming the worst, and it only fed my anxiety.

We have all walked into a room and felt like everyone was staring at us, judging our every move. Or maybe we texted someone, and when they didn't respond in three or four business seconds, we were sure they hated our guts.

This is mind reading. It's a thought pattern that both drives and is driven by our anxious feelings. Mind reading is like playing detective without any clues, leaving lots of room for error. Our brains do this to detect and predict threats, but it's not very accurate. This means we create make-believe threats more than discovering actual ones, causing very intense anxiety.

Our brains are wired to make sense of the world around us so we feel safe. We pick up on cues and gather as much information as possible.

This can be harmless and even useful in social situations. For example, when we see someone smile, we usually assume they're happy. But **when we're anxious, we tend to see things in a negative way.** We might think someone is smiling to hide another emotion or because they're going to make fun of us, instead of just saying hello.

> *People with anxiety tend to be very sensitive to social cues and interpret them as negative.*
>
> — DR. EDMUND J. BOURNE

Our brains are designed to care deeply about what others think. We have a desire to be accepted and liked by others. We want to fit in and be seen in a positive light. When we don't get clear feedback from other people, our anxious minds fill in the gaps, usually with negative ideas.

This is a **cognitive distortion**, a mental shortcut that our brains take, that's not always accurate. Instead of asking or finding out what others think, we jump to conclusions, often assuming the worst.

This triggers our body's stress response, releasing adrenaline and cortisol, the chemicals that make us feel on edge, because they were designed to help us deal with physical threats. This keeps us on high alert, which is exhausting and leads to chronic anxious feelings. Instead of simply being careful, we're spiraling into hypervigilance and paranoia.

This is a loop of catastrophic thinking that we're better off being aware of, and there isn't a magic light switch to turn it off.

Mind reading, when done correctly, isn't mind reading at all. It's about picking up on social cues, and that can be useful. For example, noticing someone's aggressive body language or slurred speech in a bar lets you know it's time to walk away. Or if you see someone fidgeting, looking around the room, or checking their phone, it might indicate they're losing interest, and you should wrap up your story.* However, we can't solely rely on social cues and need to gain more information through direct communication.

We're better off asking for clarity than making assumptions because when we fill in the gaps, we tend to make things more negative than they really are. We do it because it gives us a sense of control, which feels safer than being vulnerable and asking questions, but it's a faulty way of protecting ourselves.

We've got to challenge our inner wannabe psychics and remember that we can't know what others are thinking unless we ask. Direct communication is the best way to understand others and ease the anxiety that comes from making negative assumptions. So, the next time you feel tempted to fill in the gaps, pause, take a breath, and ask for the clarity you need.

This is easier said than done, and maybe, in my case, all those years ago back in Brooklyn, I didn't have to ask the kind ginger man why he was staring. I could have simply given him an inviting smile, and let him read between the lines to come have a slice of "home."

* Like that story about that time you thought you saw a giant gerbil, but it was just a puffy-faced puppy having a reaction to a bee sting. That plot twist just didn't hit like you thought.

WE CAN'T KNOW WHAT OTHERS ARE THINKING UNLESS WE ASK.

HUMBLE THE POET

31.

HABITS

HELPING OTHERS WITH ANXIETY CAN GIVE US ANXIETY

Friends would reach out to me for help, and it'd give me anxiety. I'd offer my best advice, they'd ignore it like an IKEA instruction manual, and surprise, surprise—their problems stuck around like that one drawer I never quite figured out how to assemble. This left me drained and disconnected from people I cared about. Helping others with their anxious feelings shouldn't mean I need to feel their anxiety too. Then I realized that maybe my approach to helping them was the problem.

I'm guilty of always trying to be a fixer. Whenever someone I care about seems full of anxious feelings, I pull out my endless supplies of solutions and advice. Sometimes I'll hit them with a playful, "Do you mind if I mansplain this real quick?"—only to find out later I'd just thrown a gallon of gasoline on their anxiety bonfire.

"Here's what you should do . . ." It's so much easier giving advice than taking it (says the guy writing this book). The reason for that is we're not doing the work, and we don't have to deal with the outcome. I'll admit it, I go back and read my own books and think, "That's some really good advice. I should try that sometime . . . not today, but sometime."

We all want to help, and some of us think our need to help comes from being super empathetic and sensitive to the needs of others. But sometimes it's not; sometimes the reason we want to help, and choose the wrong ways to help, is because *hearing someone's feelings can make us feel responsible for them.* Of course, it's amazing to help someone with their needs, but it can't always be at the expense of your own. That's a form of self-abandonment and a potent ingredient in the recipe for anxious co-dependent relationships.

Helping someone with anxious feelings is worth doing, but we have to remember that it's a delicate dance between offering support and offering solutions (they're not always the same thing), while not generating more anxiety for ourselves. The goal is to help them manage their emotions to a less-distressing place, and a to-do list of opinions, solutions, and ways to hijack the conversation rarely helps.

Here are some tips for helping others with anxiety without adding to your own:

Ask more questions

The best way I've found to help someone sharing anxious feelings is to start by asking, "Are you looking for solutions, or do you just want someone to listen?"* This simple question clarifies the type of support your friend needs. It's not always about fixing things. *Anxiety doesn't mean something is broken; it just means alarms are going off and need attention.*

Sometimes your friend may need a safe space to vent without judgment, helping them gain insight and clarity. Other times, they might want a shoulder to cry on to release their emotions. Or they could be seeking a detailed plan of practical solutions. We won't know unless we ask, and when we ask and get an answer, we need to believe them.

Empathy doesn't require you to understand a person's feelings; it just requires you to believe it. True empathy involves believing in their experience, even if you can't relate or haven't walked in their shoes.

This is the part where I remind you that empathy and sympathy are different things.

Sympathy is looking at another person's problem from *your* perspective.

Empathy is trying to authentically look at their problems from *their* perspective.

When someone falls and scrapes their knee:

Sympathy says, "Oh, I'm sorry; I can imagine that must really suck for you."

Empathy says, "Oh, I can't imagine how you feel. Getting injured is tough. Do you want to talk about it? Is there anything I can do to help?"

---

* A.k.a. nodding sympathetically and saying "That sucks' for the next hour."

It's important to remember that the way people express their anxieties and seek support can be different based on who they are. Some might mainly seek to be heard and understood, while others might be more solution-oriented. I rarely want to vent. If I'm telling you my problems, I want other perspectives, solutions, insights, and opinions.

If my friend is upset because their last social media post didn't get enough likes, even if I don't care about that stuff, it doesn't make their anxious feelings any less valid. I don't have to understand why this is important; I just have to believe it's important to them and be there in any capacity they need.

Think of it like this: if your friend is drowning in a sea of worries, they'd rather have a life jacket (support) before you cannonball in with a 12-point rescue plan (solutions). The choice is theirs, not yours. Running in with a rescue plan may overwhelm them, while support can help clear their thinking and calm them down, empowering them to improve their situation themselves.

Listen

Listening is tough. It's hard to stay focused, hard to relate, and hard not to take over the conversation. My rule for effective listening? I'm only allowed to say three magic words: "Tell me more."

These three words can help unlock deeper emotions and anxieties. They show the other person that you genuinely want to understand and are willing to listen without judgment. "Tell me more" can bring out hidden feelings that need to be heard and create a safe space for someone to vent and release built-up stress. By simply listening, you offer the rare gift of showing you truly care.

Being a great listener isn't just about being silent and nodding along. It's about being emotionally available and fully present. If you're distracted or not emotionally engaged, you can't provide the support your friend needs.

Don't plan your weekend, daydream about your crush, or look around the room. Be present. If you have to think about anything, focus on helping them identify the names of their feelings.

Reassurance

Once you've heard everything your friend has to say and there's nothing left to tell, it's time to offer reassurance. Remind them that anxious feelings are normal and there's nothing wrong with them for feeling this way.

Putting words to emotions is magic. Research shows that naming our feelings can activate calming parts of our brains, which helps reduce anxiety.

Think of it like this: if your friend is overwhelmed by a mountain of work, their stress is climbing to Everest heights. By helping them name their feeling as "stressed" or "overwhelmed," you help them understand what's going on inside, which can be surprisingly calming.

It feels good to be needed, but we have to avoid falling into co-dependency. Co-dependency is like getting stuck in someone else's emotional quicksand—you both end up sinking.

It's important to believe in your friend's feelings, but taking on their emotions as your own isn't helpful. It might feel good at the moment, but it doesn't help your friend learn to handle their own challenges. Instead of trying to be a martyr or a hero, offer support in ways that are healthy and sustainable.

Anxiety isn't just a personal issue; it's something we all deal with as a society. The more we talk about it and support each other, the better we can manage anxiety, both individually and as a community.

Anxiety thrives in isolation.
To conquer it, we need to create
a community of support.

— BRENÉ BROWN

EMPATHY DOESN'T MEAN YOU HAVE TO UNDERSTAND SOMEONE'S FEELINGS; YOU JUST NEED TO BELIEVE THEY'RE REAL.

HUMBLE THE POET

32.

HABITS

WHY TRY TO FIT IN WHEN YOU WERE BORN TO STAND OUT?

Look at the back of this book at my "I totally just got caught off guard" photo. You know, the one where I'm pretending to laugh like I've just heard the funniest joke, but really I'm thinking about what I'm going to eat later. Give yourself a few seconds to absorb my handsome beard,* and then tell yourself: "This guy fits in everywhere."

Think about how nearly impossible it is for someone who looks like me to fit in anywhere, unless we're talking about the "Getting Randomly Screened at the Airport Club." Not only am I a member, but I've got frequent flyer miles, a VIP pass, and I'm probably the president of the club.

We all want to belong, we all want to fit in, and that desire can create a lot of anxiety. This need to fit in is programmed into our human programming. For thousands of years, we've had a biological need for belonging in tribes to survive and that still drives our desire to fit in today.

Humans haven't evolved nearly as much
as we like to think we have . . .
we're still social primates at heart.

— **ROBERT SAPOLSKY**

* Not-So-Humble the Poet.

Back in our tribal days, sticking together meant survival. If you were kicked out of the tribe, you were on your own—facing hunger, predators, and a bunch of other dangerous situations. Rejection was basically a death sentence. These days, it's not as extreme, but getting kicked out of the group chat can still feel just as devastating. Even though rejection doesn't equal death anymore, our survival brains haven't caught up, and it still stings like it does. We crave acceptance, and when we get rejected, it can feel like a personal flaw, something unfixable. This fear often pushes us to fit in so much that we lose sight of our authentic selves.

This fear has us confusing "fitting in" with "belonging." Think of yourself as a piece in a giant puzzle. Fitting in means forcing yourself to change shape just to squeeze in somewhere, while belonging is finding the spot where you naturally fit, without having to bend or break who you are.

True belonging doesn't ask us to change who we are; it asks us to be who we are.

Once we begin to prioritize belonging over fitting in, a lot of the anxiety will go away.

I've bent over backward trying to fit in with people I didn't naturally vibe with. I laughed at jokes I didn't find funny and held back my true thoughts so I wouldn't offend anyone. To be honest, I probably let most people call me Humble so they wouldn't struggle with my actual name, Kanwer. I thought these compromises were necessary to achieve what I wanted or to feel like I mattered. We've all done this in some way.

What I didn't realize was that even when fitting in helped me reach my goals, it was taking me further away from who I really was. That kind of personal betrayal brings its own anxieties, and no prize or outside validation can make it feel worth it.

Fitting in means wearing a disguise—literally and metaphorically—and that disguise is always changing depending on who we're around. The masks we wear to fit in are exhausting, and after a while, we forget who we are underneath. Fitting in is temporary, but belonging is permanent. When we focus on finding where we truly belong, the only expectation we need to live up to is to be our authentic selves.

Anxiety and tension come from trying to be who we think we should be, while relaxation comes from embracing who we really are.

I came across this idea that self-hate might actually be our real self trying to break free from all the masks we wear. It's not that we hate who we are deep down, but we hate who we think we *have* to be to fit into the world. We hate how we're always being overly polite, avoiding conflict, or pretending to like stuff we don't. Whether or not this is 100 percent true, it's something worth thinking about the next time you catch yourself feeling that self-hate creeping in. Most of us don't enjoy holding back who we really are, and that frustration often fuels our inner critic.

The goal here isn't to strip off all your disguises* and run around the streets in nothing but a smile. It's more about finding ways to be your real self more often, and easing some of that anxiety that comes from trying to fit in. That starts by surrounding yourself with people who accept you as you are—but that only works if you actually show them who you are.

We all have situations where we have to put on a mask—whether it's at work or social events where being totally authentic isn't always an option. And that's okay. Sometimes you've gotta play the game for the greater good. It's not because these places are bad; it's just that in bigger groups, individual needs often take a back seat to keep things running smoothly.

> *The crowd requires conformity so it can feel safe;*
> *the individual requires nonconformity so [they] can feel free.*
>
> — SOREN KIERKEGAARD

Being yourself means constantly exploring who you are and protecting what you find. That comes with self-compassion, self-reflection, and setting boundaries that teach others how to treat you. And if you're looking for a community that accepts your authentic self, the best way to find one is to build it. Create a space where people feel free to be who they are.

* . . . and clothes.

We hear a lot about diversity and inclusion as buzzwords, but true inclusivity isn't just about tolerating differences—it's about celebrating them. Celebrate the people who think, love, pray, vote, eat, and live differently from you.

We all have anxiety about being accepted, and a lot of that comes from not fully accepting ourselves. So, let's start there. The more we understand the unique puzzle piece we are, the easier it is to find where we truly belong instead of forcing ourselves to fit in.* And when we prioritize true belonging for ourselves, we can create spaces where others feel safe to be themselves too—no extra security checks required.

* Like finding the last corner piece of a 1,000-piece puzzle. Finally things start to make sense!

THE ONLY WAY PEOPLE CAN ACCEPT THE REAL YOU IS IF YOU SHOW THEM THE REAL YOU.

33.

ENVIRONMENTS

EVERYONE'S A SOCIAL BUTTERFLY . . . IN THE RIGHT GARDEN

Picture this: You're at a party where everyone's laughing, dancing, and living their best life. Meanwhile you're glued to the wall, gripping a half-empty cup of who-knows-what, wondering how soon you can bail and cuddle your pet on the couch.* If that sounds familiar, before slapping the *social anxiety* label on your forehead, consider the idea that *you actually are a social butterfly, but you're just in the wrong garden.*

When we feel lost, self-awareness is our best guide. Who are we, really? Are we introverts pretending to be party animals or extroverts avoiding real connections? I recently learned about ambiverts—people who are both, depending on the situation. But before labeling ourselves, we should ask: What truly matters to us? What are our values and passions? What excites us? By reflecting on these questions, we can better navigate social interactions.

Saying we're not good in social settings adds to our anxiety. Instead, let's find out what environments make us feel like social butterflies and which ones clip our wings. Knowing this helps us make choices that match who we are, reducing anxiety, and making social interactions more enjoyable and authentic.

* Or spouse—whatever floats your boat.

Finding Your People

Every interaction either recharges you like a triple-shot espresso or leaves you feeling like you've been hit with the world's longest Monday, just wanting to slide into a drain like a cartoon puddle. The difference often lies in what we're talking about. For instance, I'm not a Harry Potter fan—I fell asleep during the first movie. My lovely editor Allison isn't a fan of my purposely incorrect references to get under people's skin.* But if you're a fan, imagine being in a room with others who share that passion versus explaining what a Gryffindor is to someone like me.**

It's more fulfilling to be around people who connect with us on a deeper level than those who don't share our interests. Finding our people—those who light us up instead of draining us—starts with knowing ourselves. When we understand our own values and passions, we can seek out social settings and connections that truly energize us.

"But, Humble, I like reading books, watching reality TV, bike riding, snake charming, partying on Wednesdays, and ancient pottery collecting. How am I going to find a group of people who like all those things?"

Well, my handsome friend, It's totally fine to have different friends for different things. Just like you have different clothes for different occasions, you can have different friends for different activities.*** I have a dog crew, an artsy bunch, an entrepreneur squad, and even a gang of single guys for nights out. You don't need to mix all your groups.**** It's not about finding the perfect group, but to understand that we'll feel less anxious around people who share some of our values. It's way easier to be yourself in spaces you actually want to be in, instead of trying to fit in rooms you never wanted to enter in the first place.

Being a part of different friend groups is a great way to avoid tribalism, where our whole identity becomes tied to one group, leading us to dislike everyone else we consider the "other." So, enjoy your diverse interests with different circles and see how it eases your social anxieties.

* Dumbledore's the furry guy that hangs with Han Solo, right?

** I assume it's some device to connect your phone to a computer, right?

*** including that hoodie to hide in when you're just over everything.

**** The idea of cross-contaminating friends gives me anxiety.

Watch Out for Mental Traps

Our survival brains are wired to keep us alive, not for winning popularity contests. This means we often fall into mental traps—like thinking everyone's judging our every move or that their silence means they hate us. These are just tricks our brains play to keep us out of new situations, thinking it's keeping us safe. But these tricks actually make us feel more anxiety. It's like seeing the world through a distorted lens, leading to misunderstandings and difficulties in social situations.

For some, especially those with ADHD, there's something called **rejection sensitive dysphoria** (RSD). This is when our fear of being disliked gets so intense that we start to feel it even when it hasn't happened. A small comment, joke, or gesture sets off the RSD alarm bells, making us think everyone hates us.

Think about how often you actually notice or judge others at a party. Even if you do, it isn't for long. Most of the time, we're all sharing the same insecurities and are too busy wondering if others are judging us to judge anyone else.

Social Isolation Can Feed Social Anxiety

Our social skills are like a muscle—if we don't use them, we lose them. Remember that first big gathering after COVID? It probably felt awkward. Hiding out in our rooms is the perfect setup for social anxiety. It's like being stuck on an island where the only neighbors are your own insecurities, and before you know it, they've built an entire town of "What Ifs" and "Why Me's."

The less we interact with people in REAL LIFE,* the harder it becomes to be social, and the more our survival brain starts whispering scary stories about how horrible monsters are hiding in every social corner, waiting to eat or reject us, whichever feels scarier.

Your Shade on the Social Anxiety Spectrum

Social anxiety isn't an on/off switch; it's more like a spectrum. Some people feel better in small groups and avoid big gatherings, while others thrive in large crowds but get nervous in one-on-one situations. Understanding where we fall on this

* Your phone doesn't count.

spectrum helps us figure out how we shine socially. By recognizing the people and environments that suit us best, we can socialize more comfortably and build meaningful connections.

There are no perfect socialites; some of us have just had more practice than others. Everyone has awkward social moments—it's a universal human experience, like tripping in public or forgetting someone's name. The difference lies in who decides to dust themselves off and keep going versus who lets it define their entire social life. What makes human interaction real is when it's messy, and that's also what can make it funny and enjoyable.

Here are some strategies to feel less socially awkward and melt that anxiety:

- **Social audit:** Keep a social diary and note down interactions that make you feel energized versus drained. You'll start noticing patterns.
- **Virtual:** Remember, socializing doesn't always have to be face-to-face. Online communities can be a great **starting point**,* especially if going out feels overwhelming.
- **Passion power:** Joining groups or clubs that align with your interests is a social cheat code. It's easier to chat about something you love with people who already love it too.
- **Small gatherings:** If giant crowds are too much, start small. Game nights, book clubs, or coffee meet-ups can be less intimidating.

Remember, **the bravest thing we can do is be authentically ourselves,** awkward moments and all. After all, the world needs your unique sparkle, so don't dim your light!

Lastly, what's helped me a lot in large groups is to find someone and make it my goal to make them more comfortable, taking the focus off me and how I'm feeling. I realized very quickly that we're all really in the same boat, and knowing I wasn't the only one anxious at a gathering did wonders to melt it away.

* The keyword is starting. Let's not turn this into a crutch.

YOU MIGHT ACTUALLY BE A SOCIAL BUTTERFLY, JUST IN THE WRONG GARDEN.

BLANK PAGE OR SECRET PORTAL?

You think this is just a printing error? Think again.
Scan the QR code for bonus chapters and prove
you're smarter than everyone else who skipped it.

PART 6:

NAVIGATING ANXIOUS STORMS

34.

HABITS

WE CAN'T ESCAPE WHAT WE DON'T FACE

Consider this a judgment-free zone. I'm not here to judge your life choices; I don't always make the best choices myself.* The goal of this chapter is to make you aware of how some choices can help or hurt our journey to feel less anxious.

I'm Punjabi, and like many other cultures, we have a unique relationship with alcohol. A lot of us grew up watching our fathers drink, and access to the liquor cabinet was as easy as quietly opening a door when no one was home.

Now, I have friends and family in their 30s who feel like alcohol has taken over their lives. The common thread among them is that they never stopped to think if drinking was helpful or harmful; it was just part of the norm.

But it's not just alcohol. When we're anxious, substances can feel like the quickest way to hit the snooze button on the alarms blaring in our heads. The relief is real but short-lived, and often the anxiety comes back even stronger once the substance wears off. Yet we keep going back for that temporary relief.

This isn't just about alcohol; it applies to caffeine, weed, cigarettes, prescription meds, and even substances still considered illegal.

I'm not here to judge how you've been coping. I just want you to feel better for longer.

Anxious feelings can be hard to manage, and we'll often do whatever it takes to escape them. Whether it's feeling sad, lonely, or stressed, we reach for quick fixes to numb the discomfort. Sometimes it's social pressure making us feel like we need

* I've definitely eaten cake for breakfast and justified it as "starting the day sweet."

substances to fit in or be accepted. Then there are the everyday stresses of life that drive us to substances for quick relief.

But **once we start using any substance, anxiety becomes tied to the withdrawal.** When it wears off, we're often in a worse place than where we started, and need another hit just to escape the cycle. Addiction is the shrinking of what gives us pleasure.

The attempt to escape from pain
is what creates more pain.

— GABOR MATÉ

A few years back, I had a back injury. It was the worst pain I ever felt, and after three visits to the doctor, I was given the opioid Percocet. It was the first time I ever took an opioid, and after trying it, I immediately understood why rappers were making songs about it. Those Percocets literally turned the volume down on everything that hurt in life, not just my back.

Other people even asked me if I had extra. They saw Percocet as a good time, and I don't blame them. It felt amazing, and it's not even the strongest opioid out there. A few years later, me and Percs reunited after I got some wisdom teeth out, and I can confidently say that I don't blame anyone for wanting to feel that nice all the time.

My sister had an emergency cesarean with her first child and joyfully recalls when they pumped her full of morphine. Prescription painkillers exist for a reason, but sometimes, once we get a taste, we don't want to stop.

According to the National Institute on Drug Abuse, four in five new heroin users started out misusing prescription painkillers. I don't blame anyone who gets hooked on these substances that can bring us relief.

The point here isn't about ranking substances or figuring out which ones are worse. This chapter is about realizing that the so-called "magic" pills or quick fixes we use for anxiety don't always work out as planned. Dependency can lead to addiction, and addiction is when you can never get enough of something that almost works;

that can mess with our lives in major ways. And when we don't have access to our go-to substance, withdrawal kicks in, often leaving us feeling even more anxious than before.

I love weed, but I'm not lost about the toll it can take on a person.* The goal here isn't to turn you all into Sober Samanthas who only drink water, have no social life and scream obvious lies like "I get high off life." The goal is just to help us all become more aware and more empowered when dealing with our anxious feelings.

Substances are like hitting the snooze button on anxiety—they quiet the noise for a bit, but they don't stop it. To really turn off that alarm, we've got to let ourselves feel what's going on inside. Our brains might crave that temporary escape, but relying on substances keeps us from building the resilience and growth we need to handle life's challenges.

If we deal with anxiety by giving ourselves unhealthy rewards like stimulants, our brain will learn that being anxious gets us those treats. Eventually, we'll start craving anxiety just for that quick relief.

Instead of just using substances to cope with anxiety, we'll feel better training our survival brains to handle it in healthier ways. That means practicing real, everyday choices—like moving our bodies, eating better, and getting enough sleep—to help us feel good overall. Simple practices like deep breathing, and bringing yourself back to the present with mindfulness practices will really help with stress and anxiety too. It's also important to build social connections that don't revolve around substances. And remember, talking about your feelings with people you trust—a friend, family member, or therapist—goes a long way in helping you deal with anxiety in a healthy way.

Before you run to dump all your liquor and pills down the toilet, let's take a beat. Going cold turkey usually ends with you staring at an empty bottle, googling "how to un-dump things from a toilet." Instead, let's focus on managing the anxiety we get around the substances we ingest and take baby steps from there. It's about gradually reducing reliance on these crutches while building up our own resilience and coping mechanisms.

* Just ask any stoner who's lost 45 minutes trying to remember why they walked into the kitchen.

Maintaining healthy habits means knowing your own triggers. I've learned which situations make my anxiety spike and which friend hangouts usually end with one too many bad decisions. If I want to make healthier choices, I've got to limit how often I'm in those situations. It's about setting myself up for success. To make positive choices, I need to set boundaries on how often we hang out.*

I also have a gang of sober friends, and activities with them revolve around nice dinners, stretch sessions, and therapy talks in the sauna, and even early-morning dance parties.**

It's always easy to medicate, distract, and avoid anxious feelings, but we can only do it for so long before everything comes tumbling down. We've seen it happen to our loved ones, and some of us already know it's happening to ourselves. Remember, we're not here to escape anxiety; we're here to listen, learn, and manage what it's trying to tell us so we can continually grow and have new experiences, which makes life worth living. We can't do that if we're always living in a foggy haze, distracting and medicating ourselves from all the messages life is sending us.***

* I still love y'all, just in small doses.

** Shout-out to Daybreakers.

*** Like: "Call your mom back," or, "Maybe not that third plate of nachos."

WE'RE NOT HERE TO ESCAPE ANXIETY; WE'RE HERE TO LISTEN, LEARN, AND MANAGE WHAT IT'S TRYING TO TELL US.

HUMBLE THE POET

35.

REACTIONS

A SHATTERED HEART CAN BUILD A STRONGER YOU

There's a restaurant bar two blocks from my place in the city that I stumbled upon late one night. The energy was amazing for a random weekday—a mixed crowd, everyone was friendly, and it became my go-to spot after a long night of adventures.

Then one day, I popped in, and the woman at the reservations desk hit me with, "It'll be a two-hour wait." My local entitlement flared up as I tried to figure out what the hell happened. Turns out, they got reviewed by a big publication and were now ranked the second-best bar in all of North America. The place was packed, and suddenly, I was on the outside looking in.

This was my most recent heartbreak.*

Going back into my memories of heartbreak, I have no idea how I made it through them. I couldn't give myself the advice that those experiences would make me stronger, because decades after my first true romantic heartbreak, I still experience them, and they still suck.

Heartbreak often seems like a clean, sad crack down the middle when we talk about it later, but in the moment, it feels like a brutal punch to the heart, shattering it into pieces. The pain is raw and overwhelming, like your chest is being crushed, leaving you gasping for breath.

Whether it's a breakup with a boyfriend or girlfriend, a falling-out with a close friend, or finding out your local bar is now too cool for you, the emotional pain is intense and overwhelming.** It feels like our heart is literally breaking, and the anxiety that

* For some reason, "It'll be a two-hour wait" stung more than a "We need to talk" text.

** Except the bar didn't leave a hoodie or scrunchie behind for me to sniff when I miss them.

comes with it can make it hard to think, breathe, and just exist. I can't make those feelings go away, but I can help explain what's happening so you can observe and eventually surrender to them as they happen.

A study from the University of Michigan used brain imaging to find that the same areas of the brain that light up when we're physically hurt also activate when we experience emotional pain. Helen Fisher, a biological anthropologist, has done research that's shown that when we're rejected in love, there's an increase in activity in our dopamine system. **You're actually more in love when you can't get somebody than when you can.** Heartbreak kicks our survival brain—the amygdala—into overdrive, slamming the alarm and telling us we're in danger. That's when all those anxiety-inducing chemicals start flooding in, making us feel fear and panic. Meanwhile, our logical brain—the prefrontal cortex—loses its grip on the situation, leading to impulsive decisions just to quiet the alarm. Maybe that means eating a whole tub of ice cream while hate-watching *Friends* because somehow everything reminds you of your ex, or heading out to drink enough to forget your own Netflix password.

Heartbreak causes us to worry about the future, feel insecure, and obsess over what went wrong.* Fear of the unknown is a big part of this anxiety. After a breakup, we feel anxious about what comes next, and the uncertainty about our future is daunting. Heartbreak also shakes our self-esteem. We start questioning our worth and wonder if we'll ever find love, friendship, or another bar** again. On top of that, losing someone important leaves us feeling isolated and alone, which amplifies anxious feelings.

Observing what's happening in our brain and body without judgment—that's my favorite definition of surrender. Letting these feelings run their course helps us manage the pain and anxiety that come with heartbreak. The more we try to snooze those unpleasant feelings, the stronger they get. So instead of pushing them away, let's acknowledge them. Accept and validate what you're feeling. It's okay, and necessary, to feel sad, angry, or anxious without judging yourself for it. Feeling your feelings is part of healing.

* It also makes you wonder if deleting all your ex's photos from Instagram was too soon or not soon enough.

** I'm sorry, but their appetizers were so good!

In short, **stop trying to skip the sad songs on your emotional playlist. Just let them play.**

> *Whatever you're going through, treat it as if it was an active decision on your part.*
>
> — **ECKHART TOLLE**

Pretend it was all part of your master plan. Ask yourself: If I hadn't had my heart broken, what's another reason I would have left that relationship?

Exploring this question puts us in control, shifting our focus from helplessness to a new perspective. It challenges us to look at how the relationship didn't match our values or needs, helping us realize that maybe its end has some silver linings. This shift in thinking allows us to see the breakup as an opportunity for growth, rather than just a loss.

It's not a magic pill to make all the pain go away, but it'll help you make progress in the right direction.

Sharing our feelings with friends,* family, or a therapist will also provide relief and help us process our emotions. Just talking, or writing it out, will make a huge difference. And of course, taking care of our bodies through eating, sleeping, and living will also improve our mental health.

It's important to mourn the loss of a relationship—they're what make life worth living—but that doesn't mean we can't create new ones during that process. Isolating ourselves when our hearts are broken is pouring salt in an open wound. Let's prioritize finding new ways to connect with others. Join a club, take up a new hobby, or reach out to other friends.**

Also, let's give ourselves time before making any big decisions. Our brains are dealing with a lot, and taking a step back can help us think more clearly. Remember, *it's okay, and normal, to feel heartbroken and anxious*. By feeling our feelings,

* As long as your friend doesn't respond with, "I saw it coming," because then you'll just need a new friend and a bigger tub of ice cream.

** Even the friends you ghosted when you started that relationship.

taking care of ourselves, and getting outside support, we can navigate this challenging time and come out stronger on the other side.

Personally, and don't take this as gospel or science, but what helps me is remembering that a broken heart is an open heart. When we're hurting, it's a chance to share those shattered pieces with the world. Sure, this can sometimes explain unhelpful rebound behaviors, but on the flip side, it can also mean using that energy to volunteer, help others, and focus on bringing value to the people around us. It's about taking that pain and turning it into something that connects us with others.

As someone who's racked up enough anxiety-inducing heartbreaks that my next one is 50 percent off, I've learned that even with a discount,* they still hurt just the same. But I've also found that shifting the focus away from myself and toward serving others makes the healing process smoother. **Helping others takes the spotlight off our own pain and gives us a fresh sense of purpose and connection.** It redirects our energy, helping us find meaning in unexpected places, and keeps us from getting lost in our heartbreak.

As for that bar, I went back after a few weeks, completely anxious that I'd be turned away again. But to my surprise, they recognized me and went out of their way to find me a spot. The rush had died down, and I realized they weren't too good for me after all. I guess this isn't really a story about heartbreak, but more about my toxic on-and-off relationship with a local bar. So, maybe you can disregard this chapter and just wait until the person who broke your heart falls off the cool list and suddenly has time for you again.

* Use my promo code: BrokenHeartedBeard143

OUR BROKEN HEART IS AN OPEN HEART.

36.

HABITS

MORE MONEY ≠ LESS ANXIETY

When I was 16, I found a part-time telemarketing job that paid more than minimum wage—meaning I made more money than my older sister, who was scooping ice cream at the mall. In my teenage mind, I was pretty much a billionaire. During the colder months,* I worked as much as I could to stack up money. Every paycheck that winter, I'd budget a certain amount to spend and put the rest in savings. But as things warmed up outside, I was working less and spending more.

Then I learned about NSF.

I wrote a check to pay for my graduation photos, and after a few weeks, I was told it bounced and that I'd be charged an extra $25 penalty as a result of "nonsufficient funds" or NSF.

This was my first experience with anxiety around money. Even though I felt like I was rolling in cash, I was far from it. I wasn't tracking my spending, and it got out of hand. I was treating myself like every day was my birthday—new clothes, gadgets, and always paying extra for guac. And, of course, things only went downhill from there.

This would be a theme in my life, especially when I earned more.

Fast-forward to my adult life: I quit my job and steady paycheck of being an elementary school teacher to pursue creativity full time, and dug myself into almost six figures of debt.

* A.k.a. most of the time in Toronto.

I was flat broke in this era of my life, and I couldn't afford to avoid my money problems anymore. Before I figured out ways to make money, I had to address my spending. I got rid of my car, stopped buying clothes, and no longer went out to eat or had any fun. I even cut up my credit cards and paid for everything in cash. These responsible money habits stuck with me as I started earning more money, and it put me in a good space to not put myself in a hole ever again.

During the worst of those times, I didn't do taxes for six years. I thought the government was going to lock me in jail and make me donate my hair to pay off the debts. Then I started working with an accountant, who told me my situation wasn't anything unique, and a lot of people choose avoidance when they're financially overwhelmed.

Money is a source of stress, anxious feelings, and helplessness for almost everyone. Whether you have a lot or a little, it's a complex relationship that we often oversimplify, thinking the solution is "I just need to make more."

Many of us turn to "retail therapy" to numb our anxieties. I'm not here to judge anyone; I always pay extra for guac when I'm at Chipotle. We just have to remember that **spending more money to relieve the stress of not having enough is like dipping your Band-Aids in hot sauce before putting them on your cuts.** Remember, you save 100 percent when you don't buy anything.

Money is important, philosophically and practically. It shapes our options, influences our choices, and dictates our sense of security, and unfortunately, for many it's a measure of self-worth. We have to respect this reality before we can take any steps toward creating a healthy relationship with our finances.

A lot of us stress over money, not simply because we don't have enough but also because trying to understand it feels like reading a physics textbook upside down.

Money is like a language, and its vocabulary and grammar can feel confusing and overwhelming. Most of us weren't taught how to speak it in school, and talking about money is often seen as taboo in social settings. Mix that with a culture that screams, "Buy stuff, be happy," and a world of cashless transactions* and it's easy to see how we're being set up for disaster.

* It's easier to spend money when you don't see the money flying out of your pocket.

Nobody starts with the same hand in the game of life. We come from different economic backgrounds and face unique challenges, all of which shape the way we experience anxiety around money.

The world is tough—job insecurity, rising living costs, student debt, and all kinds of financial struggles naturally add to our stress and anxiety. **It's completely normal to feel anxious about life's challenges,** but if we let that anxiety go unchecked, it can stop us from improving our situation.

A lot of us grew up facing trauma and hardship, and those past experiences with financial instability or loss can leave emotional scars. These scars trigger anxiety even now, making us either ignore our spending and let it spiral out of control or hoard our savings, never spending on the things we really want because we're afraid it'll never be enough.

Holding ourselves to impossible financial standards and comparing our lives to others just adds to the anxiety of not feeling "successful enough." Back in the day, we only saw how our neighbors were doing, and if we lived in the same area, we were all living pretty similarly. But now, with social media, we're bombarded by people showing off their supercars, exotic vacations, and luxury strollers for their not-so-cute kids. There's this subtle pressure to keep up, pushing us to focus more on **looking** successful than actually **being** successful.

For people with existing anxiety or depression, financial worries can feel even more overwhelming. I have a friend with bipolar disorder who has to hide her credit cards during manic episodes to avoid making impulsive purchases. It's a reminder that mental health challenges can make managing money even tougher, creating a vicious cycle of stress and spending.

Growing up in an immigrant household, we were always told to pinch every penny. While that's solid advice, it only works until it doesn't. Spending an hour researching fancy beard brushes just to save $6 isn't really saving money—it's wasting time. I've had to work with a therapist to recognize and break out of my immigrant-family-inspired scarcity mindset. Survival mode isn't bad—it's a natural response—but it becomes a problem if we stay there, stuck and unable to evolve mentally or financially.

For me, the work has included realizing that **time is more valuable than money.** We can always make back lost money, but we can't make back lost time. Shifting to this mindset has done wonders for easing my financial anxiety.

Mo' Money Less Problems?

It's easy to think that being wealthy means less anxiety about money, but the truth is, financial stress hits everyone, no matter how much they have. There's pressure to maintain a lifestyle, fear of losing what's been earned, and anxiety about the future, all of which feed into financial worry—even for people who seem to have it all.

Money talks, but it doesn't tell the whole story. Assuming someone with more money doesn't have stress just fuels our own sense of helplessness. Anxiety, especially financial anxiety, is more complicated than that.

Living in New York City, I see people working themselves to exhaustion just to keep their heads above water. They think it's survival, but often it's about maintaining a certain lifestyle. The rent I pay in New York would stretch a lot further in a smaller city or even overseas. Just knowing I have options if things get too expensive helps reduce my anxiety.*

Financial Literacy

The smarter we are with money, the more empowered we feel. We live in a capitalist system that thrives when we're financially clueless and spending nonstop. We're hit with thousands of ads every day, even if we don't notice them. This constant push to earn and buy more subtly suggests we're not enough if we don't have more.

Financial literacy is about understanding the basics: budgeting, managing debt, saving, investing, and planning for the future. It's not a magic cure, but it's a powerful tool. Knowing how to handle your money gives you control, reduces anxiety, and builds security. You don't have to become a financial wizard or predict the stock market; just having the basic tools to confidently navigate your finances is enough to calm the chaos.

* Yes, moving is full of anxiety too, but so is digging an early grave working 60 hours a week to live an unsustainable lifestyle just to stay where we are.

Knowledge is power, and when it comes to money anxiety, financial literacy is your best weapon.

The D Word

Debt sucks—it's like that clingy ex who shows up at every family reunion. And no amount of deep breathing, positive thinking, or yoga poses is going to make it disappear. None of us wants to be in debt, and when bills pile up, it gets even harder to tackle. But we have more options than just playing the lottery or hiding, hoping it disappears.*

As with anything that triggers anxious feelings, we need to face debt head-on. That means listing all debts, their interest rates, minimum payments, and deadlines. It's not fun, but bringing it into the light is way more empowering than sweeping it under the rug. Debt is a fear we need to confront.

Defending yourself from debt isn't just about paying it off—it's about preventing more from stacking up. This takes us back to budgeting like a pro, tracking every dollar you spend, and avoiding impulse buys.** Every dollar you save is a brick in the fortress to protect you from the debt monster and the anxiety it vomits onto us.

The B Word

One of the best antidotes to money anxiety is structure, and that structure comes in the form of a **budget**.

As with anything that makes us anxious, we need to start by focusing on what's in our control. One of the best pieces of financial advice I ever got was, **"It's not about how much you make, but how much you spend."** It's easy to spend without realizing it, especially with subscription services silently pulling money from our accounts—whether it's TV streaming, gym memberships, or food delivery. Even using credit cards and tapping our phones to pay makes it harder to keep track.

* I've done both and trust me, they don't work.

** Retail therapy isn't real therapy—though it does come with the same bill, minus the breakthroughs.

Budgeting, as unsexy as it sounds, is a superpower that works wonders in reducing money anxiety. **A budget isn't a prison—it's a road map for the future we want.** It helps us see where our money is going, cut back where we need to, and plan for unexpected expenses. Since anxiety often comes from uncertainty, a budget puts us back in control, giving us less to worry about and preparing us for those "what if" moments.

Like a lot of things that make us anxious, we tend to think we're the only ones feeling it, and we should be embarrassed. Trust me, you're not alone—it's normal to have anxiety, especially around money.

My accountant was a lifesaver in helping me realize my financial problems weren't monsters, and we could deal with them. Budgeting apps can be a huge help, and there are support groups out there too. Talking about your money problems can feel like showing someone your Internet search history—awkward and a bit terrifying. But once it's out there, you'll feel lighter, and the advice you get might be worth more than finding discount codes for your favorite store.

Often it's simply about having access to the right information. Not all of us grew up in families that knew about managing money, and that's okay. It's never too late to seek it out and learn from others.

> *The hardest part about being broke is pretending like you're not.*
>
> — **MARILYN MONROE**

I wouldn't claim to be a stock-picking expert or act like a financial planner, but building a foundation of knowledge and taking those first steps can set your future self up for success. Saving something is always better than saving nothing, and the act of saving alone teaches discipline and brings its own rewards. The math is simple: put money away now, and you'll have more later. Keep it slow and steady—no one gets rich quick, and that's okay.

A friend once told me that the only way to feel abundant is to share, and that stuck with me. If money isn't buying happiness, maybe we're not spending enough on others. As my finances improved, I found myself in new circles with people who had more, and instead of feeling anxious about keeping up, I shifted my mindset to giving more. Whether it's extra cash for someone in need or investing in others' dreams, sharing what we have brings a sense of fulfillment.

At the end of the day, what's the point of all the financial literacy, budgeting, and being debt-free if we can't pay it forward?

Do you love buying stuff to deal with your anxiety? If you lied and said no, while your online cart is bursting at the seems, scan the QR code to check out this bonus chapter titled: BUY SHIT, BE ANXIOUS.

OUR WORLD ISN'T DESIGNED TO HELP US FEEL SECURE WITH OUR MONEY; IT PUSHES US TO EARN MORE, BUY MORE, AND FEEL LIKE WE'RE NEVER ENOUGH.

HUMBLE THE POET

37.

HABITS

HOW DO WE FEEL OUR FEELINGS?

When anxious feelings creep up on me, I tend to go full ostrich—sticking my head in the sand—or more accurately, into my phone, snacks, and an obsession with fixing up my apartment. It usually starts on a regular day when I wake up with that weird knot in my stomach. To bury the worry, I grab something to eat right away. And of course, I can't eat without watching TV, so I turn on something easy to watch, like a mindless show.* Eventually I get so fed up with Amy and Jake's "will they or won't they" nonsense that I switch to FIFA, where at least my virtual soccer team is reliable . . . until I lose and have to remind myself not to throw the controller across the room by turning back to my phone.

While doom scrolling, I see a video of a guy being hit on by a beautiful woman, and my mind starts spiraling. Why doesn't that ever happen to me? Is that even real? Why is there a camera? I snap out of it, but now I'm fed up with the TV, my phone, and my snacks. But that knot in my stomach? Still there.

So, in my quest for distraction, I hop on Amazon and grab a few more pointless things for the apartment—because, obviously, you can never have too many floating shelves and baskets to organize all the stuff you don't really need but suddenly can't live without. Maybe another walk with the pup will help. Four walks in for the day, and yet, that uneasy feeling just won't budge.

All day, I'm doing different things to snooze the knot in my stomach until they make things worse, but why's that knot there in the first place?

* Currently *Brooklyn 99* for the fourth time.

For a long time, I thought my anxiety was there to haunt me, but it's not. It's there to tell me something, and the reason it won't go away is because I'm doing everything except listening to it. **Anxiety is often our body's reaction when we can't connect with uncomfortable emotions.** When we avoid feelings like sadness, boredom, fatigue, anger, or disappointment, anxiety signals that something within us needs attention. Distraction and avoidance aren't failures; they simply mean we haven't learned to sit with discomfort. Once we can face these emotions without running, we move from distraction to progress.

Let's say, instead of running from the feeling, we decided to listen to it. How do we do that? How do we listen to a feeling?

Well, we feel it.

It sounds simple, but actually sitting with our feelings isn't easy or fun. Let's be real—feeling our feelings sucks. That's why we've built whole industries around *not* dealing with them. From social media to endless snacks, substances, and Netflix shows we pretend to watch *ironically,* we're always trying to escape. We'll pay top dollar just to avoid feeling what's really going on inside.

When we avoid our feelings, they grow. The world is full of distractions to temporarily bury, dampen, and turn down the volume on anxious, uneasy feelings. But bottling it up, medicating, and avoiding it only works for so long. We're delaying the inevitable.

The least we can do is feel these feelings on our terms instead of when we've run out of ways to temporarily snooze them (a.k.a. hit a breaking point).

But how do we actually feel? What are the steps to feeling something, especially something we don't enjoy feeling?

Let's start with the easiest step:

1. Identify the sensation beneath the feeling

We've all had that sinking feeling in our stomach when we're nervous or felt a burst of energy when we're excited. These are sensations our body picks up. But when we give them meaning—like calling that sinking feeling "anxiety" or that burst of energy "excitement"—those sensations turn into feelings.

Take a moment to scan your body and pay attention to any sensations that line up with your emotions. Do you feel a knot in your stomach, tightness in your chest, tingling in your legs? These are all clues to where you hold your emotions.

Feelings are just the labels we give to these sensations, shaped by our thoughts, memories, and beliefs. The same sensation can be felt differently depending on the situation. That flutter in your chest and the surge of energy? It could be excitement if you're looking forward to something good, or anxiety if you're dreading something. It's all in how we interpret it.

Our body also plays a big role in this with hormones like adrenaline and cortisol. Adrenaline gives us that jolt of energy, while cortisol helps us deal with stress. Understanding how these hormones work can give us better insight into why we feel the way we do.

2. Name the feeling

A game-changer in my life has been discovering the emotion wheel. It helps find better words to explain the feelings we have.

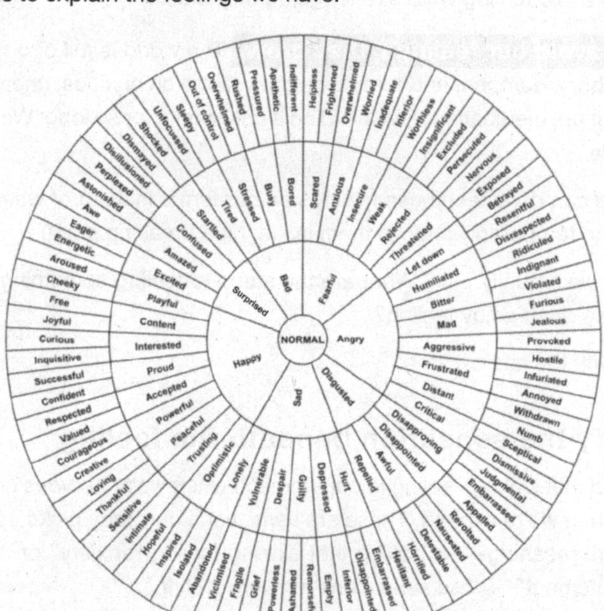

When we can name our feelings, we take away some of their power to control us. Instead of saying, "I'm anxious" or "I'm overwhelmed," we can change the language to "I'm feeling anxious" or "I'm feeling overwhelmed." This shift allows us to remember that we're experiencing the feeling. Naming it as specifically as possible helps bring clarity and reduce the intensity of that emotion.

3. Breathe through the feeling

Here's where things get magical. This ancient practice that our ancestors and other creatures have done for millions of years can improve how you feel. It's called BREATHING.

Take slow, deep breaths, focusing on inhaling and exhaling fully while focusing on where you feel the sensations. This simple act can help calm your nervous system, reduce the intensity of your emotions, and bring you back to a state of balance. Breathing helps us reconnect with our bodies and feelings, and unlike that gym membership we're too anxious to cancel, it's completely free and incredibly effective.

We take a breath for granted and take shallow breaths when we're operating on autopilot. But when we take deeper, more intentional breaths, we'll quickly improve how we feel.

If we can breathe into an uncomfortable feeling for 90 seconds, it'll start to fade. Only 90 seconds. Try it now. Close your eyes, focus on your breath, locate the sensation, and let the feeling wash over you.

Our feelings come and go in waves, so when the wave is hitting, it's a sign to get more intentional and deeper with the breathing.

Take a few deep breaths, and allow yourself to experience the emotion without judging it.* Go deeper, hold it longer, and let it out slower; try to exhale slowly for 7 to 10 seconds.

While you're doing this, you can also gently rub the area you feel the sensation, give yourself a massage or a hug. All this, combined with the breath and awareness, will help the wave of the feeling take its course.

* Remember: it's okay to not feel okay.

4. Accept the feeling

We often judge our feelings as "good" or "bad," but in reality, all our feelings are simply messages. Joy helps us connect with others, sadness allows us to grieve losses, and anger can motivate us to take action. None of these feelings are the enemy—they serve a purpose and highlight things that need our attention.

Suppressing feelings is like trying to hold in a sneeze: it might work for a second, but eventually, it's going to come out in the most embarrassing way possible. Showing emotions doesn't make us weak; expressing emotions is a sign of strength and self-awareness. ***There's beauty in an ugly cry.****

The goal isn't to change our emotions but to observe them. Observing doesn't mean we're approving of those emotions; it just means we're acknowledging them and giving them space without judgment. I like to think of emotions as hotel guests. Some guests might trash the room, while others leave it better than they found it. Our job is to welcome each one, do our best to accommodate them, and clean up afterward.

When we resist our emotions, it often makes them stronger and likelier to stick around longer. It might feel like a good short-term fix to push them away, but it has consequences later. By letting our feelings flow naturally, without resistance, we build a healthier relationship with all the emotions that come our way.

5. Learn from the feeling

Once we've created space to accept our emotions, we can observe and reflect on them to choose wise and graceful responses. Ask yourself:

- *What's this emotion trying to tell me?*
- *How can I respond to it in a helpful way?*

This practice also allows us to look at how we've been coping with and avoiding these feelings. How often were we running from them? What were our go-to distractions?

* It took me a long time to realize this.

Recognizing our triggers is another crucial step. ***Emotions are records of our past experiences,*** so when you feel a trigger, ask, "How does this relate to my past?" For example, whenever I see a German Shepherd, I'm reminded of my first dog, Himmatt, who passed away after 11 amazing years. One time in a park, I saw a dog that looked exactly like Himmatt. My body seized up, and I couldn't move. I was triggered by the trauma of losing someone special, and my body reacted as if there was a threat, putting me in freeze mode.

Understanding our triggers means we can also change them to create new pathways for behavior. This can be as simple as changing your phone wallpaper, rearranging your living space, or breaking patterns in your daily routine. Altering triggers helps reduce the sting of unpleasant emotions but isn't a replacement for facing and feeling them.

It sounds basic, but feeling our feelings is the only secret to having a better relationship with them. We have to understand them, name them, breathe through them, accept them, and learn from them.

6. Keep breathing through the feeling

Two deep breaths in through the nose; one long breath out the mouth.

Accepting your emotions doesn't mean you like them.
It means you're not afraid of them.

— SUSAN DAVID

I still catch myself with my head firmly in the sand,* but I'm quicker to notice it and start this process of feeling these feelings. Some days are easier than others; sometimes the knot in my stomach is a conversation I don't want to have, but every time I decide to lean in to it, I realize I need to distract, avoid, and medicate much less moving forward. Progress matters, and all we're here to do is get a little bit better than we were before.

* Humble the Ostrich.

THERE'S BEAUTY IN AN UGLY CRY.

HABITS

38.

BEAT UP YOUR ANXIETY WITH BOREDOM

My mother used to take us to the gurdwara, the Sikh place of worship, every night during the summers. In Toronto, some of these gurdwaras were in old department stores, others in office buildings, and one was an old portable classroom. The community would do their best to make it feel like a slice of Punjab. The singing of hymns, the food, the community, the gossiping aunties, and the decor could transport you out of Canada for a moment, and I understood why my mother wanted to be there so often.

I, on the other hand, dreaded going. I couldn't understand what was being said, but I had to sit there and listen. I would have preferred playing outside with my friends to pretending to listen to adults sing hymns and discuss philosophy in a language I barely understood. This was before phones, so my options were to sit in the langar hall (free kitchen) and slowly drink tea, or sit at the back of the main hall and let my imagination run wild. It was there that I learned boredom could be my best friend.

As a kid, almost everything felt boring, but it sparked some of my most creative moments. When there wasn't much to do, I'd let my mind roam, creating whole imaginary worlds and stories to fill the time. It was how I dealt with the monotony, turning those endless hours of nothing into something fun.

Fast-forward to adulthood, and boredom looks different. Modern life makes my survival brain feel like it's at a rave I didn't RSVP for.* My phone is always sending

* Flashing lights, booming sounds, and a vague sense that I should have stayed home in sweatpants.

notifications, and I jump from one thing to the next. I'm so constantly stimulated that it's become an addiction. I crave it. I need it as soon as I wake up and to fall asleep. My days feel like a nonstop adrenaline rush. It's exciting, but in this endless chase, I've become a prisoner of my own anxiety.

Today's constant stimulation is a huge source of anxiety. We're always trying to be entertained and engaged, leaving little room for introspection and peace. We've become dopamine addicts, chasing the next thrill to numb feelings we should be addressing. **This endless search for stimulation is taking a toll on our mental health.**

But what if we stopped? What if we embraced boredom the way we embrace cheat days on a diet?* Instead of seeing boredom as an enemy, we could view it as a space for introspection, creativity, and, most importantly, relief from anxiety.

Boredom lets our minds wander and explore parts of ourselves we usually ignore. In these quiet moments, we can connect with our deepest desires, work through anxious thoughts, and remember the simple joy of just being alive. Danish philosopher Søren Kierkegaard said, **"The cure for boredom is curiosity."** When we look at boredom as a chance to get curious, it can actually help us manage anxiety. It's about finding peace in those quiet, still moments, away from all the noise and distractions.

Don't think of boredom as doing nothing or missing out. It's more like a blank canvas where your imagination can create its own masterpieces instead of constantly taking in everyone else's. As an artist, boredom is my best friend. Sitting in it helps me tune in to the whispers of inspiration. That's how writers find their voice, how scientists stumble onto discoveries, and how we build a better relationship with ourselves. If you want to go far in life, learn to be comfortable with boredom, silence, and being alone—these quiet moments build patience, focus, and inner strength.

I'm not asking you to become a hermit, toss your phone in the toilet, and cut off all human contact.** It's more about finding balance—moments of quiet within the

* Sure, it's not exciting, but it's oddly satisfying once you get into it.

** Though if you've ever dropped it in there by accident, you know that might be a blessing in disguise.

busyness. Start small: take a walk without your phone and listen to the sounds around you. Sit in silence for a few minutes each day, just observing your thoughts without judging them. If we want a deeper adventure into the universe within us, we need time away from the digital world outside us. At first, your body will scream for a dopamine hit, but sit long enough, and that craving will fade.

Lately I've been trying something different: covering my eyes, taking a few breaths, letting the anxious feelings pass, and just sitting with the stillness. Some sessions go better than others, but one thing's clear—being bored on purpose is way more nourishing than I thought.

The biggest adventures of my life aren't in the chaos of the outside world—they're in the quiet corners of my own mind.

Silence is the language of God;
all else is poor translation.

— RUMI

It costs you nothing to try being bored. Start small—one minute a day for a week, then bump it up to two. After a month, you'll be at five minutes of nothing. After a year, you might find yourself comfortably sitting in an hour of quiet. Doing nothing for that hour will ease your anxiety and add so much more beauty to the remaining 23 hours of your day.

The stories little Humble told himself while sitting in that corner of the gurdwara, watching people while slowly sipping his tea, shaped him into the curious, bearded man he is today. His latest curiosity is anxiety, and I hope his work is helping you feel just a little more unanxious.*

* This first-person/third-person younger Humble vs. older Humble is confusing me too. Let's just all smile and nod.

IN THE QUIET MOMENTS, WE RECONNECT WITH OUR DEEPEST DESIRES AND START TO UNTANGLE THE KNOTS OF ANXIETY.

HUMBLE THE POET

39. IS THAT ANXIETY IN YOUR GENES, OR ARE YOU JUST HAPPY TO SEE ME?

As a Sikh* I carry a history that's filled with both incredible resilience and deep trauma. Sikhi started in the 1500s by Guru** Nanak Dev Ji, who spoke out against the rulers of his time for their human rights abuses. He was imprisoned for it, and his resistance sparked a movement that encouraged Sikhs to get involved in their communities and challenge those in power. By the 1700s, this movement had grown into both a spiritual and military force. Over the centuries, our people faced repeated attempts to wipe us out, with mass killings that shaped our identity as fighters and survivors.

Growing up, I saw paintings and photos of these brutal times, showing different rulers claiming different faiths and nations, all aiming to suppress our community. It wasn't until I was older that I realized how many situations triggered anxiety in me, echoing these past traumas. Yes, the strength of these warriors and heroes is in my blood, but so is the trauma.

You don't need to be aware of your traumas to feel the anxiety they cause. Often we experience anxiety without knowing its source. Sometimes the trauma that triggers our anxiety is so deep that we don't remember it. Other times it's hidden in plain sight, embedded in our DNA, quietly influencing us.

* Sikh = Student

** GU = Dark, RU = Light, a guru is an enlightener or teacher. I would not be a "self-help" guru, I would be a "How to keep your beard shiny" guru.

This is what we call generational trauma and anxiety.

Yes, our anxiety isn't just triggered by things from our past or worries about the future; it can also be sparked by experiences our ancestors had long before we were born.

Until we acknowledge the pain and suffering of the past, we cannot truly heal the wounds of the present

— IYANLA VANZANT

Think of it like inheriting an old, worn-out backpack filled with stuff you didn't pack—and might not even realize you're carrying. Each item in the backpack represents the trauma your ancestors went through: the fear your grandparents felt during war, the anxiety your parents faced as immigrants, or the stress of living in a hostile society. You're carrying this heavy backpack everywhere, not knowing how much it's weighing you down or affecting how you move through life. These burdens don't just disappear—they shape how you handle everyday situations and how you react to the world around you.

Research shows that trauma can be passed down not just through behaviors but also biologically—a concept called **epigenetics**. This means trauma can leave chemical marks on our DNA, affecting how our genes work without changing the DNA itself. These marks can change how we handle stress, making our bodies react more intensely to things that feel threatening.

In her research published in *Biological Psychiatry*, epigenetics expert Rachel Yehuda found that children of trauma survivors—descendants of Holocaust survivors, for example—often have different levels of stress hormones like cortisol. These changes in stress response suggest that trauma experienced by one generation can make the next more likely to struggle with anxiety and stress. So, **some of the anxiety we feel today might actually come from the trauma our ancestors went through,** making us more sensitive to stress, even if we haven't experienced that trauma firsthand.

Generational trauma and anxiety show up in all kinds of ways—like how our survival instincts go back to our ancient ancestors or how we've inherited our mom's habit of being extra cheap.* Some of this anxiety is just part of being human, while other parts are tied directly to where we come from.

Take communities that have gone through big historical trauma—things like slavery, genocide, or colonization. People from these backgrounds often carry the weight of their ancestors' struggles. This can show up as anxiety, depression, substance abuse, or having a hard time building healthy relationships. It's not just something from the past; that trauma still lives in us today.

On top of that, ongoing discrimination and feeling marginalized add even more pressure. It leaves people feeling isolated, powerless, and constantly on edge—all things that make anxiety worse. In these situations, the survival brain is stuck on high alert, always looking for danger even when there's none. That overdrive makes us more anxious, seeing threats that aren't really there.

Charlamagne Tha God does an amazing job exploring cultural PTSD in his book *Shook One*, showing how the fears we inherit from past generations shape our daily lives and decisions. He says, "Cultural PTSD isn't just about the traumatic events; it's about how those events shape how we see ourselves and each other today." It's a reminder that a lot of the anxiety we feel now is tied to past trauma. We might avoid things that bring up old pain or struggle to relax because of nonstop, anxious thoughts.

The point isn't to get stuck in victimhood but to dig deeper into why we feel this anxiety. **It's not about blaming our ancestors** but recognizing that their experiences still affect us.** Once we get this, we can understand our fears better, show ourselves some compassion, and find ways to heal. By seeing these inherited struggles, we can start to address them.

Inherited trauma doesn't have to be a life sentence. Facing those uncomfortable feelings, instead of running from them, is how we start to gain control. One powerful way to heal is by reframing our story—seeing those inherited traits as strengths

* I got it from my Mama.

** But fuck those who marginalized, oppressed, and traumatized them.

instead of burdens. They might make us more empathetic, more aware, or more in tune with others.

Building new habits is key. Just like trauma gets passed down, so does resilience. Focus on shaping your thoughts and actions based on who *you* want to be, not who others say you should be. And remember, you're not in this alone—therapy, support groups, or just talking with friends and family can make a huge difference.

Cultural PTSD might be part of our past, but it doesn't have to shape our future. By facing these inherited fears and anxieties, we can heal not just ourselves, but also our communities. Our mind's strength is one of the most powerful tools for growth.

I wear my turban tall and let my beard grow long because, for a long time, looking like me was a death sentence. So many communities have been oppressed just for being different, and that pain doesn't just disappear. The point of this chapter isn't to make us feel sorry for ourselves, but to recognize that we carry this in our bones—and to celebrate how far we've come. It's about passing down our generational resilience to the next generation.

But here's the thing—politicians who want power and profit know this pain can be used against us. They'll exploit that trauma, making us feel unsafe and blaming "others" to keep us divided. It's an old divide-and-conquer trick, designed to make us look to them for solutions to problems that were never really there.

Yes, your trauma is real, but don't let anyone use it to make you turn against others. **We didn't survive monsters only to become them ourselves.**

YOU DON'T HAVE TO BE AWARE OF YOUR TRAUMAS TO FEEL THE ANXIETY THEY BRING.

THIS BLANK PAGE BROUGHT TO YOU BY BUDGET CUTS

Just kidding—we saved some good stuff for the QR code. Scan it and enjoy some bonus chapters while this blank page pretends to be useful.

PART 7:

BUILDING EMOTIONAL STRENGTH

HABITS

40. UNTANGLING ANXIETY BEGINS WITH ASKING FOR HELP

Here's a story no one knows about me except one of my sisters.*

This is the time I had to cut a large chunk of my hair off.

Back when Darwin, the Ikea Monkey, warmed our hearts, I was a year into leaving my stable job as an elementary school teacher. I was just realizing that the opportunities I thought would get me paid weren't happening and probably never existed.

This meant intense dread of having no idea what I was going to do. I was drowning in debt, and I had no idea how to make any money. It didn't look like anyone was going to swoop down from the sky to fix it all for me.

I felt hopeless.**

When we're feeling hopeless and trapped, anxiety can hit hard, making us think there are no options left and we're stuck. Sometimes this leads us to neglect simple things we usually take care of. For me it was combing my hair.

* And probably the other, considering they tell each other everything, but I'll only find that out after this book is out.

** Like Millennials and Zoomers trying to own a home in this economy.

I was in full-on shutdown mode and stopped caring for myself. Instead of brushing my hair, I just kept wrapping it up in layers of cotton and tying a turban on top. Over time my hair turned into one giant, tangled mess. It wasn't stylish like those cool, intentional hairstyles. It looked more like a bird's nest that had survived a hurricane, a rock concert, and a wrestling match with a wild raccoon*—all at once. It seemed like it had its own plans, maybe even for world domination.

The more it got out of control, the more anxious I felt, and the more I avoided dealing with it.

It seemed hopeless, a giant symbol stuck to my head of the life I was living, from the stupid decision of quitting my job to chase my dreams. I thought the only option left was to go nuclear, cut it all off, and hope that, as a man in my 30s, it would grow back. This was a frightening idea, as keeping uncut hair is something I was raised to value in my Sikh heritage.

Ironically the solution to improving both my life and the jungle on top of my head was asking for help.

Even though I had felt helpless for so long, I knew asking others for help was an option, but I was just too scared. The thought of it raised my anxiety, playing ideas in my head that people would judge me, criticize me, and make me feel bad for the life choices I made, and make me feel gross for what lived on my head.

I went to my older sister Gurbir and asked her for help.

To my surprise, Gurbir didn't run out screaming when she saw my hair—she just gave it a good ol' "Hmm" like she was diagnosing a stubborn math problem. After taking a look, she calmly said, "Oh, that's not too bad, have you tried conditioner?"

To which I replied, "Does 2-in-1 count?" At this point, all you women reading this are screaming at the heavens your disdain for 2-in-1, 3-in-1, and the mythical 6-in-1 body washes.**

Over the course of that evening, we got some high-quality conditioner, and we worked on the hair, softening it up, making it a little bit easier to comb some out.

* Rest in peace, Conrad. #DeadRacoonTO

** Cleans your left arm, right arm, body, left leg, right leg, face, and hair, also serves as a shampoo, dish soap, and surface cleaner combo that men inexplicably trust.

When she worked on it as much as she could, things were a little better; it wasn't perfect, but we made progress. She gave it her best, but it was clear this was a job for a professional—someone trained in both hair and crisis management.

The next day we went to her salon, where she explained to the hairstylist my situation. I was nervous and still ashamed, and my hair was completely covered. The stylist was warm and gentle when she spoke to me. She realized this wasn't simply about working on hair. My sister explained that we wanted to salvage as much as possible without having to cut anything, and the stylist worked her magic.

Once again, after seeing my hair, the stylist didn't have any response, she didn't make me feel gross, she didn't even have to reassure me of anything, she did something even better; she treated me like a normal everyday client.

I was still anxious and couldn't even look at myself in the mirror. I think the stylist noticed and made small talk, and my sister sat there, chatting along with us.

After an hour, she had made a lot of progress detangling my chaotic clump, and that process wasn't as painful as I thought. When she did all she could, she said the rest would have to be cut. I took a deep breath, made eye contact with myself in the mirror, and said, "Let's do it."

I had to cut off about a quarter of my hair that day, much less than the whole lot, but more than I ever thought I ever would in my life. As she snipped away, I felt a rush of emotions come up, not just about my hair, but about myself, who I was, and where I was taking my life. I had to fight the urge to cry while it happened, and there are tears in my eyes while I type this.

After she was done, I assessed the damage. There were no bald spots, no tragic comb-overs in my future, just a full head of smooth, shiny hair—though I definitely felt about five pounds lighter and maybe 20 percent less stressed. Not fully relieved, and still very ashamed, I tied my hair back up in a turban, paid and thanked the stylist, and left the salon.

My sister gave me tips for washing my hair with separate shampoo and conditioner moving forward, and over a decade later, I still hear her voice every time I wash my hair:

"Scratch your scalp, get all that dead skin out."

"Be really generous with the conditioner, cover every inch, use more than you think, and leave it in there."

My despair and anxiety came from thinking I didn't have any options. I thought my only choices were to live with this tangled tumbleweed rolling around my head, or having to shave it all off, and with it, an identity that I valued so much.

But the moment I gained enough courage to ask my big sister for help, more options appeared. There wasn't any judgment, and years later I look like Gandalf's* younger, cuter little brother with my hair flowing down my back.

There might be a knotted mess on top of your head right now, and it may feel like you've run out of options, and that despair, that hopelessness, is filling you with an overwhelming anxiety that is making the problem even worse.

Realize the despair comes from feeling like we've run out of options, not the problem itself.

What I'm here to tell you is there are always more options, and the best way to find them is to ask for help.

Asking for help isn't easy; it means being vulnerable, and that's scary.

When we're vulnerable, we're showing people ways to hurt us. I already felt gross with my hair, I couldn't bear being judged for it, and the truth is I can't promise you that those worst-case scenarios won't happen. My sister could have said, "Eww." The hairstylist could have gasped in horror and run out of the salon. But that doesn't change the fact that more options revealed themselves when I put myself out there.

> *"Vulnerability is not knowing victory or defeat; it's understanding the necessity of both; it's engaging. It's being all in."*
>
> —BRENÉ BROWN

* He was in Harry Potter, right?

Whether my hair problem was addressed or not, I was amplifying my anxiety by hiding from it. Expressing what was scaring me started the uphill spiral to improving my situation and how I felt about it.

So if you're feeling anxious and hopeless, go hunting for some more options, using your vulnerability as a compass.

Years later, during the pandemic, I went to support a friend's sister's underground hair salon to help her keep afloat during lockdown.* I hadn't been to a salon since that time with my sister, but I remember how nice the head massage and hair wash was.

As I sat down and let my hair out, the first thing my friend's sister said was, "Bro, you need to brush your hair more."

Old habits die hard.**

* Is it okay to snitch on myself?

** Especially when it comes to haircare. I swear, every time I reach for a bottle of 2-in-1, I can hear Gurbir's voice yelling, "DON'T DO IT!"

FEELING HOPELESS DOESN'T MEAN THERE'S NO WAY OUT; IT MEANS WE HAVEN'T ASKED FOR HELP YET.

41.

REACTIONS

WE CAN TRAIN OURSELVES TO DEAL WITH ANXIETY

My first day of jiujitsu was terrifying. I didn't know anyone, and I got paired up with a brown belt—someone with at least six years of experience, who could probably fold me into a pretzel before I even knew what was happening. This was for my first sparring match, or "roll." In jiujitsu, rolling is all about controlling your partner's body and making them submit. How? By choking them, twisting an arm or leg in a painful way, or, if all else fails, tickling them into surrender.*

My first roll felt like getting tossed into a human washing machine—limbs flailing, sweat everywhere, and me frozen, wondering if there was a pause button. I had no idea what I was doing, and my opponent was completely in control. A few weeks later, nothing had really changed. I was still getting submitted and choked out, waiting for that magical moment where I'd suddenly get better.

But **improvement didn't come from winning matches—it came from feeling calmer** during the rolls. My survival brain started to understand when I was actually in danger versus when I was just uncomfortable. Things began to slow down, and I wasn't wasting as much energy, but I'd still freak out and scramble whenever I found myself in a situation I didn't recognize.

* I might have made that last one up.

A year in, I can now roll with a smile on my face,* even when someone's trying to twist my arm into a pretzel. Progress, right? I'm not that much better skill-wise than I was on day one, but I'm way calmer and more aware. This calmness slows everything down, helping me catch on to what my opponent's trying to do, and I freak out way less. I've even become a commentator during rolls, making my opponent laugh as I regularly shout, "Ah shit, you got me!"—like it's a friendly chess match, not an attempt to choke me with my own gi.

What I've done over those months is basically graduate from the **Shutdown** response to **Panic**, and now I'm hanging out in the **Chill** phase of anxiety, as described in **polyvagal theory**.

> *The polyvagal theory offers a road map for healing trauma and building resilience.*
>
> — STEPHEN PORGES

We all know anxiety feels like trash—sweaty palms, trouble breathing, butterflies in the stomach, and that cold, shaky feeling—but what's actually going on inside our bodies and brains? We often talk about being in fight-or-flight mode, but there's a bit more to it. Understanding how our nervous system reacts gives us some clarity on how to handle anxiety better.

Think of your body like a phone with a battery that reflects your nervous system's state.

- **Chill mode (social connection):** Imagine sitting in a café, having a great convo with your best friend. You're relaxed, your heart rate steady, and you're connected and happy. It's like your phone is fully charged and ready for anything. This is your body's default mode when things are calm and safe.
- **Panic mode (fight-or-flight):** Picture walking alone at night, and you hear footsteps behind you. Your heart starts racing, your palms get sweaty, and you're on high alert. You're ready to either confront whatever's coming (fight) or run away (flight). Your phone's battery is

* Mainly because I'm wearing a mouthguard.

low, and it's shutting down nonessential apps to save energy—logical thinking and calm decision-making are some of those "apps."

- **Shutdown mode (freeze):** Now imagine someone pulls a gun on you. You're so overwhelmed that you freeze—unable to speak or move. Your body has hit a hard stop, like a phone that's completely out of battery. This is your last-ditch effort to conserve energy when facing serious danger.

None of these modes are the bad guy. They're survival tools we've evolved to have. The problem is, in today's world, the Panic and Shutdown modes get triggered by everyday stuff—deadlines, awkward texts, public speaking. Even when there's no real danger, our bodies react like there is. Understanding these modes helps us know what's happening inside, so we can respond better.

Our best self shows up when our logical brain, the prefrontal cortex, is running the show. Here's what it does for us:

- **Thinking ahead:** It helps you plan, whether it's picking the next move in a game or figuring out how to solve a problem.
- **Controlling your emotions:** When you're excited or upset, the prefrontal cortex helps you stay calm. It's like your brain's built-in therapist, offering wise words when emotions get intense.
- **Making good choices:** It helps you weigh right from wrong, guiding you toward the best option, even when it's tough.
- **Learning:** When you're learning something new, this part of your brain is like a teacher, helping you absorb and understand information.

But **when anxiety kicks in, our logical brain takes a backseat,** and our survival brain jumps in, saying, "Don't worry, I got this!"* This shift makes us less rational and more primal. Suddenly we're reacting to non-dangerous situations like they're life-or-death. This is why we say or do things we don't mean, communication breaks down, and everything feels harder than it is.

The survival brain isn't our enemy; it's just trying to protect us. Think of it as that one dramatic relative at Thanksgiving who shouts, "Fire!" when there's just a little

* Spoiler: It does not have this.

steam coming off the mashed potatoes. Relax, it's steam, not a five-alarm fire. We don't need to evacuate the house.

Our default as humans is to be on alert for danger—it's been that way for over a million years. We've got three stages to react to threats, but our internal alarm system hasn't really caught up to the modern world, so we have to tweak it ourselves. **The goal isn't to silence the stress or anxiety but to listen and respond to it properly.**

When you feel stressed, check if you're in **Chill mode**, **Panic mode**, or **Shutdown mode**, and take steps to bring yourself back to safety. Simple mindfulness practices, like doodling or deep breathing, can help. Next time you're feeling on edge, try taking five slow, deep breaths to help ease yourself back toward Chill mode.

Remember, our body freaks out when it doesn't think it has the energy to handle things. The simplest ways to recharge are exercise, drinking more water, and getting some good sleep.*

Exposing yourself to stress sounds weird, but it's like training for the stress Olympics—practice makes things easier. Eventually, that last-minute "urgent" email from your boss won't feel like a disaster. You're teaching your Panic and Shutdown responses to chill out, and that helps your brain stay in control. The more you face stress calmly, the better you get at handling it.

Rolling in jiujitsu has helped me manage stress in other parts of my life. Work meetings don't freak me out as much, and social events aren't so overwhelming anymore. Even confrontations feel more manageable because I've learned to stay grounded. Trying new things is less intimidating too, thanks to the mental toughness I've built up.

When we stop seeing stress as the enemy and start viewing it like a sparring partner, it gets easier to handle. This builds confidence and gives us a sense of control. Anxiety usually comes from fear and feeling out of control, but the more stress we handle, the stronger we get, and the less we'll slip into panic mode.

Don't get me wrong, I love being lazy and taking it easy. But I've learned that tackling hard things makes other hard things easier—especially when life throws

* Turns out the secret isn't five cups of coffee injected directly into your veins.

curveballs. It's all part of the process, and that's okay. Celebrate the small wins and progress, and you'll start facing the world with more confidence and less anxiety, spending more time in Safe mode.

I'm still a white belt in jiujitsu as I write this, but I'm aiming for blue.* Apparently, at blue belt is when the learning really starts, but I already see how it's helped me find calm in chaos with a more managed nervous system.

This means less tickling too.

* So be my accountability buddy and send me a message, checking to see if I earned that beautiful blue yet.

THE MORE STRESS WE HANDLE, THE STRONGER WE GET, AND THE LESS WE'LL SLIP INTO PANIC AND SHUTDOWN MODE.

HUMBLE THE POET

42. IT'S NOT SELFISH TO PUT YOURSELF FIRST

I realized recently that since I don't broadcast the challenges I face in life, it makes others think that I don't have any. That, combined with the fact that I'm considered a self-help author, leads people to think I'm an emotional superhero and I can be an endless source of support for them. Don't get me wrong: I don't mind helping people now that I'm in a position to lend some money and have the time to lend an ear. This turns into a problem when I'm not taking care of myself and don't have the bandwidth to be there for others; we can't pour from an empty cup.

I'm sure you've felt the same.

There's a price to neglecting ourselves, and self-neglect isn't simply sucking on cigarettes and brushing our teeth with cake frosting. It's also putting everyone else's needs before our own.

A Cornell study by Tom Gilovich revealed a hard truth: 76 percent of people, when reflecting on their lives, regret not living for themselves. Putting ourselves first is important for our well-being, but we often fear looking selfish, so we push our own desires aside to please others. We might even romanticize this as being selfless, and when we start to feel stressed or burned out, we justify it by thinking we're being martyrs for a cause.

Don't be a martyr; take care of yourself first. By ensuring your own well-being, you're better equipped to support others effectively.

Putting our needs last leads to subtle, slow-growing types of anxiety. This kind of anxiety is always simmering in the background, and we might not even realize it until it flares up and causes unexpected damage. It feeds into our negative self-talk, making us overthink situations, second-guess our decisions, replay past mistakes, and stress about future problems. It's sneaky, disguising itself as stress, fatigue, or general unhappiness. We might think these feelings are just from the daily grind or that something is wrong with us, but in reality, it's this underlying anxiety at play.

This feeling isn't the price we pay for being selfless—it's burnout. Ignoring our own needs drains our energy, and in the long run, it keeps us from truly helping others. This isn't our fault. Society bombards us with messages that glorify being selfless, making us feel guilty for even thinking about our own happiness. But that story is incomplete. Helping others is great, but we can't do it if we're running on empty. **Constantly putting others first isn't a badge of honor; it's a one-way ticket to burnout.**

Putting others' needs ahead of your own is often painted as a noble act, but constantly being the emotional support system without taking care of yourself, or shelving your dreams to meet others' expectations, only leads to burnout, regret, and resentment.

When we bail out friends and family members without boundaries, we not only harm ourselves, but we also do them a disservice. Overextending to make everyone happy puts us on a path to manipulation, exploitation, and difficulty expressing our own needs.

Whether it's taking on extra work, staying in a job we hate, lending money we don't have, or going into business with friends who show red flags, these are just a few ways we feed our anxiety by neglecting ourselves. This pattern only drains us further and makes it harder to break free.

Brendon Burchard described our inbox as just an "organized list of other peoples' priorities."* We must realize that what we choose to prioritize defines our lives and, if those priorities are not our own, how much of that's chipping away from us.

* In my case it's also a graveyard for "I'll get back to you later" ghosts.

So how do we protect our time and ourselves, minimize this anxiety, and not feel like a selfish piece of shit?

Let's start with the one quote I always find a way to sneak into my books:

Putting yourself first isn't selfish—expecting others to put you first is.

— HUMBLE THE POET*

Say that 10 times as you work toward these next steps:

- **Acknowledge Your Needs:** Your well-being matters. Taking care of yourself isn't selfish—it's necessary.
- **Set Boundaries:** Learn to say no when something drains you. Boundaries protect your energy and teach others how to respect your time.
- **Reframe Selfishness:** It's not selfish; it's self-respect. When you put yourself first, you're able to help others more effectively.
- **Start Small:** Make small changes, like scheduling "me time" or taking quick breaks. These build confidence over time.
- **Communicate Clearly:** Be honest about your needs. People can't respect your boundaries if they don't know them.
- **Practice Self-Compassion:** Be kind to yourself when guilt creeps in. You deserve care as much as anyone else.
- **Surround Yourself with Support:** Stick with people who respect your boundaries and support your self-care.
- **Focus on Long-Term Wellness:** Taking care of yourself now helps prevent burnout and keeps you in a better place to help others later.

Remember: putting yourself first isn't about abandoning others; it's about building a strong foundation from where you can really care for them. It's about saying yes to your own happiness, which ultimately empowers you to say yes to others in a more authentic and fulfilling way. Take the first step, however small, and watch your life blossom.

---

* Probably.

PUTTING YOURSELF FIRST ISN'T SELFISH— EXPECTING OTHERS TO PUT YOU FIRST IS.

HUMBLE THE POET

43. KNOWING OUR VALUES CALMS OUR ANXIETIES

A few years ago, I had two core memories form in the same week, both wildly different. Early in the week, I landed a national commercial for Apple, which felt like a peak moment of success. But just a few days later, a back injury knocked me off my feet, reminding me how fragile that success was compared to my health. This whole experience drove home a lesson I won't forget: it's not the outside achievements that define us, but our core values that keep us steady and calm, even when life throws curveballs.

The back injury was no joke—it felt like random jolts of electricity shooting through my body. I had to visit the ER three times before anyone took my pain seriously. That led to my first experience with prescription opioids and the claustrophobia of an MRI.

When I finally got the paycheck from the Apple job, there was nothing to celebrate. I had to use a cane just to walk to the bank, and all I could think was, "None of this matters if I don't get healthy again."

There's a popular quote attributed to Confucius: "A healthy man wants a thousand things; a sick man only wants one." And let me tell you, I wasn't thinking about any of those thousand things—I was just focused on being able to sneeze without it feeling like I'd been struck by lightning. As much as the back injury seemed sudden, it was really the final straw that *broke the Humble's back*. I wasn't taking care of myself, and it added up.

Through focusing on my health, I got better, and with the help of physio, I came out stronger and more mobile than before.

But more importantly, I realized that having clear priorities gave me a sense of clarity that reduced my daily anxiety. Before the injury, I was floating through life like a plastic bag in a windstorm—just bouncing around, reacting to things, and hoping I didn't get stuck. I wasn't sure where I was going, and that uncertainty left me uneasy. Turns out, a little clarity and a working spine can do wonders for your sense of direction.

There are times when life feels like we've been dropped in the middle of a desert with no clue which way to go, and that lack of direction sets off our anxious alarms.

It's tough when we feel like there aren't enough options in life, but **having too many choices can be its own special kind of nightmare.** We get confused, overwhelmed, and stuck—paralyzed by fear of making the wrong move. When we don't have a clear path, our brain gets overloaded by all the options, leading to decision fatigue. The paradox of choice leaves us exhausted and anxious, with our nervous system going on high alert, reacting to a threat that isn't even there. We end up feeling lost, drained, and unsure of our next step.

Sometimes life simplifies our focus, like when I injured my back. Having a clear, pressing issue, like a back injury, forces us to focus on solving it—it becomes our guiding star, whether we like it or not. That clarity makes decisions easier because the priority is obvious. But when everything is going great, we don't have those intense guiding stars. It's the everyday microdecisions—what to wear, what to eat, how to spend a day off—that can flood us with choices and ramp up our anxiety. We get overwhelmed and end up distracting ourselves, avoiding decisions, or numbing out just to snooze that anxiety.

I'm not here to tell you what to eat for lunch,* but I'll say that with the bigger decisions, having a guiding star will help.

What can that guiding star be?

* My next book will be called: *What to Eat For Lunch: Bearded Recommendations from a Guy Who Sleeps In Until 11 A.M.*

Personally, I think it should be our core values. Knowing what matters to us will help us be more clear and decisive when we hit too many forks in the road.

When I had my injury, I realized that more important than my career and my bank account was my health. This was a core value, and it wasn't difficult to put everything else on the back burner to address it.

Core values are the things that matter most to you—they're like your inner GPS,* helping to make life a little less scary. They guide you toward decisions that feel right and true to who you are, so you don't end up going in circles with anxiety riding shotgun. When you know your core values, it's easier to make choices that reduce stress and keep you grounded.

No, your core values aren't the way you eat an Oreo,** or whether you pronounce "gif" as "gif" or "gif."*** Sure, those things sort of matter, but real core values go deeper. They're about *why* you make the choices you make and what truly guides you through life.

Our core values give us purpose, which is the opposite of being aimless. When we choose a purpose aligned with our values, life feels more meaningful and less scattered. With that meaning and direction, our survival brain feels less threatened by new choices, so it triggers anxiety less often. Instead of spiraling in "what-ifs," we realize it's not about making the "right" decision—it's about making any decision right by aligning it with what matters to us. Indecision triggers anxiety because it leaves us feeling uncertain and out of control, and that's why core values are key to staying grounded.

Let's not mistake our value and purpose for our goals. We can calm our anxious feelings by focusing on values instead of goals. Goals keep us restless, waiting to feel good only after we've achieved them—and then there's always the next one. It's like running on a treadmill that never stops. But values are here for us now. They let us feel grounded and purposeful in the moment, no waiting required.

Our brains love the progress we make when we chase purpose-driven decisions. Dopamine, the feel-good chemical, kicks in when we close the gap between where

* Except this one doesn't keep recalculating every time you miss a turn.

** Obviously it's cream first, then throw away the cookies.

*** It's pronounced "gif."

we are and where we want to be. You don't even have to reach the goal—just moving toward it gives you that boost. But to make any progress, you need direction. It doesn't have to be crystal clear; even a vague direction is better than none at all.

Deciding what truly matters can be scary because it means letting go of other paths and options. It requires courage and commitment to align with who we really are. We'll have to make sacrifices and say goodbye to past versions of ourselves. For me, I had to spend more on physio and work less to prioritize my health over money. It was a trade-off, but I knew my health mattered more than being rich and broken.

When we set intentions, we create a road map for our lives. Each step brings us closer to what truly matters, and suddenly, it's like we're cruising with the windows down instead of endlessly circling the block. Being intentional about our goals simplifies decision-making, bringing clarity and easing anxiety. This structure gives our minds direction and helps those anxious feelings fade.

My therapist once told me that the satisfaction from many of my accomplishments didn't stick because they weren't aligned with my core values.

So, naturally, I asked, "How do I even know my core values?"

Here's what she said:

- **Do some soul searching:** Think about what makes you happy, proud, and fulfilled. What activities light you up? What causes do you care about?
- **Ask yourself questions:** Who do you want to be? What impact do you want to make? What would your ideal life look like?
- **Talk to people you admire:** Ask them about their values and how they live them out.
- **Don't stress about getting it perfect:** Your values can change over time, so just start exploring. Even aiming at an unclear target is better than having no target at all.

Therapy helped me realize that figuring out my core values is an ongoing adventure, not a destination. When I was injured, it was easy to focus on the one thing I valued—getting better—because everything else became irrelevant or too hard to do.

We live in a world where it doesn't always feel safe to be our true selves, but figuring out who that is matters. There's a high price—confusion and anxiety—for not knowing.

Knowing what's important to us makes it easier to say no and feel good about the path we're on. That's tough in a world full of social media, FOMO, and self-help experts telling you how to live.* But our best life is the one that's most true to who we really are. And if the most authentic thing for you is just wanting to feel healthy, that's a great place to start.

I thought the juicy Apple paycheck was the gift that week—a sign that I'd made it or was at least on the right track. But long after the money was gone and the high from my 15 minutes of fame faded, I realized it was the injury that truly changed me. It forced me to focus on what really matters before life could hit me in an even more inconvenient way.

I'm in a better place physically now, but I know that injury could flare up at any moment. That constant reminder keeps me focused on what matters most—my health. I no longer feel invincible, and now every decision I make goes through the filter of "How will this affect my health and how I feel?"

I'm not here to tell you what your core values should be. I'm just here to remind you that figuring them out is one of the most important things you can do. It helps make life more fulfilling and calms the anxiety that comes when we feel lost or overwhelmed.

Now, go stretch those hamstrings.

* The irony isn't lost on me here.

LIFE ISN'T ABOUT MAKING THE "RIGHT" DECISION— IT'S ABOUT MAKING ANY DECISION RIGHT.

44.

THOUGHTS

WE CAN'T *FIND* PEACE, WE CAN ONLY *MAKE* IT

On top of a snow-capped mountain, in a tiny hut made from recycled tree bark that died of natural causes, lives someone with a beard longer than mine who's supposedly achieved inner peace. Their breath smells like happiness, and their smile is the true pearly gates of heaven. When they speak, birds get pregnant, and their laugh gently massages your lower back.*

Yes, folks, inner peace is totally real, and you can have it. Just tell me your birthday, the three-digit code on the back of your credit card, and your mother's maiden name, and I'll whisper the secret in your ear.

Inner peace, much like my offer for it, is bullshit.

There's no such thing as everlasting tranquility, constant happiness, or a life without anxiety. The idea of always being at peace has been sold to us through social media, advertising, self-help books,** and cultural stories that promise a perfect life if we just follow certain rules or buy certain products.

Ironically, **chasing an anxiety-free life will cause more anxiety.** Trying to achieve constant peace makes us view our normal, anxious responses as failures, which then makes us feel even more anxious about being anxious, creating a vicious cycle.

Instead of trying to *find* peace, let's *make* peace. Let's make peace with anxiety, understanding it as a natural part of life and learning how to manage it constructively.

* Including that hard to reach IT Band.

** This isn't a self-help book, it's a wellness book; there's a difference. 😜

Life is hard to understand and even harder to predict, and anxiety is how our brain responds to that uncertainty. It's a signal telling us that something needs our attention, maybe something we need to act on or think about. The idea that we can completely eliminate anxiety or reach a point where nothing bothers us is just unrealistic. Anxiety is part of being human—it's an instinct that's helped us stay alert and survive danger.

At this point, you probably want to negotiate: it's not that we don't want our brain to signal us when something needs attention, it's just that we hate how the signal feels. What if, instead of the intense feelings of anxiety, we got a gentle chime, and a calming British voice whispered in our ear to focus on something important? That would be way better than the adrenaline-fueled chaos of heart palpitations, sweaty palms, and fuzzy vision.

Unfortunately, my handsome friend, when there's an actual threat, a little chime and an ASMR British whisper won't exactly light a fire under us to deal with danger right away. Anxiety is there for a reason—it's the boost of energy you get when you realize you slept in and have exactly 57 seconds to shower, brush your teeth, pluck your nose hair, get dressed, and dash out the door before you're late for school/work/interpretive dance class. That's *useful* anxiety.

Then there's the *not-so-useful* kind, like when you second-guess every little thing you say or do, convinced you'll regret it later.

Useful anxiety doesn't feel great, but it kicks us into gear when we need it. Not-so-useful anxiety? It doesn't help *or* feel great, but the good news is, we can work on that.

Society likes to sell the idea that wellness means never feeling discomfort, but **a meaningful life isn't about avoiding pain or anxiety.** It's about facing them in ways that help us grow, learn, and accept ourselves. Constant peace sounds nice, but it's an illusion that keeps us chasing something we'll never fully reach, instead of embracing what it really means to be human.

Anxiety is a normal response to life's ups and downs. Instead of trying to get rid of it, we should focus on making peace with it—accepting it as part of the human experience and finding healthy ways to deal with it. That means building resilience, practicing mindfulness, and figuring out strategies to face challenges without getting overwhelmed.

What people often mistake for inner peace is really just **equanimity**—which is just a fancy way of saying staying calm and balanced, even when things get tough. You don't have to live on a mountain or grow a beard* to have equanimity; you just need to practice managing your emotions.

What skills and habits can we practice for less stress and more calm?

Mindfulness	Accepting What's Out of Our Control	Reframing Negative Thoughts	Connecting with Others	Self-Compassion
Aligning with Our Values	Emotional Awareness	Limiting Exposure to Media	Exercising Our Bodies	Embracing Impermanence
Meditation	Gratitude	Simplifying Life	Creative Expression	Setting Boundaries
Patience	Accepting Others	Sleeping Well	Forgiveness	Eating Well

The goal of this big list isn't to overwhelm you but to give you a variety of options to explore for creating more peace in your life. You don't need to do them all. Each practice has levels, so you can start small and build over time. The idea is to find what works for you and take it at your own pace.

These habits build resilience, which gives us more control over how we handle life's stresses. Every day, we decide how to respond to our feelings and the world around us. We learn to make peace with our anxieties, our mistakes, and the things that don't go as planned. This kind of peace is realistic and doable. **It's not about eliminating challenges or reaching a perfect mindset, but finding ways to be okay even when life is messy.**

Instead of chasing some impossible idea of inner peace, we can focus on the real, tangible peace that comes from accepting life as it is—constantly learning to adapt, accept, and grow.

* Although I would love if you did. #BeardBuddies

CHASING AN ANXIETY-FREE LIFE WILL ONLY CAUSE MORE ANXIETY.

45.

REACTIONS

WE NEED STRESS TO AVOID BURNOUT

I wanted to kick off this chapter with a cute, insightful, and vulnerable story about my experiences with burnout. But honestly, my stories are more like a glitchy laptop—everything's fine until, suddenly, it's not, and I'm left wishing for the good old days of CTRL + ALT + DELETE. And now, I don't even know how to reset, so I just sit there, staring at the spinning beach ball of doom. One of my clearest memories of burnout is breaking down and confessing to a friend that I often fantasize about not existing.

I don't think I need to share too many stories for you to know we're all in the same boat when it comes to burnout. It's less about the details and more about the feeling. And that feeling is hard to describe beyond just being absolutely exhausted.

Burnout isn't just about being tired. It's emotional, physical, and mental exhaustion that comes from too much stress for too long—it's your body throwing up its hands and saying, "I'm done. Good luck surviving without me." Anxiety makes it even worse, draining your energy and making recovery feel impossible. When you're burned out, motivation goes out the window. Every little thing feels heavy, overwhelming, and impossible. It's like you're stuck in a dark tunnel, with no light at the end, and you don't even remember how you got there.

There's no shame in reaching this point. Burnout is really common these days, and it's not your fault. But by understanding what burnout is, how it happens, and what parts of it we can actually control, we can start to deal with it better.

To put it simply:

Think of your energy like a battery.

- **Stress** is like having all your apps running in the background—it slowly drains your battery over time.
- **Anxiety** is like a glitch in the battery. It messes with how your energy is stored and used. Even if you're not doing anything major, anxiety drains your battery faster than regular stress.
- **Rest & Motivation** are your chargers. They refill your battery, giving you the energy to tackle life's challenges.

When you keep using up your battery without recharging (through rest and finding motivation), you hit **burnout**. At that point, your energy is completely drained, and even the simplest tasks feel impossible.

Common causes of burnout:

- **Workload:** Having way too much to do with too little time or resources.
- **Control:** Feeling like you don't have control over your work or life.
- **Reward:** Not feeling appreciated or rewarded for your efforts.
- **Community:** Feeling isolated or unsupported by colleagues, friends, or family.
- **Fairness:** Believing you're not being treated fairly.
- **Values:** Working in a way that clashes with what's truly important to you.

So, the secret to avoiding burnout is living a life of constant naps, vacations, and deleting all stress and anxiety, right?

Well, no.

First, there's no such thing as a life without anxiety and stress, and second, stress can actually boost motivation.

Think of stress as a spice. A little bit adds flavor and excitement to your life, giving you that push to get things done. Add too much, and suddenly, it's overwhelming.

Not all stress is created equal either. There's *positive stress*—the kind that motivates you—and *distress*, which overwhelms you. Positive stress is like the buzz before a first date or the rush you feel when a deadline looms, and somehow you pull off a miracle. It helps you power through challenges. Distress, on the other hand, makes you feel out of control and feeds those anxious thoughts that keep you awake at night.

Positive stress is great when it pushes you to your limits, fuels your creativity, and motivates you. Distress drains your energy, clouds your judgment, and makes focusing impossible.

So, no, avoiding all stress isn't the answer either. The real trick is managing it. Sometimes it's not the workload that causes distress but the lack of work.* Avoiding stressful tasks in the short term only makes them more stressful in the long run.

We need just enough stress to keep us moving forward, but not so much that it overwhelms us. This is where motivation comes in.

Motivation helps us see challenges in a more positive light and gives us the energy to tackle them. It's that inner voice reminding us that what we're doing matters—and that we matter too. **When we're motivated, stress can actually become a helpful tool rather than something to fear.**

But even with the best motivation, burnout can still sneak up if we don't take care of ourselves. Ignoring burnout signs and pushing through can lead to bigger issues. Depriving ourselves of sleep, doom-scrolling for hours, and chugging seven cups of coffee won't solve anything. These habits pile on avoidable stress, making it harder for motivation to do its job. We need to take ownership of our habits and reduce the unnecessary distress in our lives to stay balanced.

Here are some things to keep in mind when it comes to managing burnout and stress:

- **Set boundaries and say no:** Know your limits and don't hesitate to hand out "no" like it's Halloween candy. Protect your energy.
- **Sleep and hydrate:** Who knew that sleep and water could be the ultimate life hacks? Get more of both and watch how they work magic on your mood.

* Hello, procrastination.

- **Manage your time:** Planning and structuring your day does wonders for your mental health. It's like giving your brain a road map instead of letting it wander aimlessly.
- **Make time for fun:** Fun isn't a luxury; it's a necessity. Schedule time for things you enjoy, whether it's hanging with friends, diving into hobbies, or just chilling. **People who plan their fun are actually more productive.**
- **Switch up your environment:** Break the monotony by working from new places. A change of scenery can do wonders for your motivation.
- **Prioritize self-care:** Healthy eating, sleep, exercise, and activities you enjoy aren't indulgences—they're essential. Take care of your physical and mental well-being.
- **Take breaks:** Recharge throughout the day with short breaks for movement or even deep-breathing exercises. A quick reset can keep burnout at bay.
- **Break big goals into smaller tasks:** If a big goal like "write a book" feels overwhelming, start by writing one sentence. Still too much? Just open the Word doc—it's a win.
- **Stop comparing yourself*:** Comparing yourself to others** is the fastest way to feed self-doubt. Focus on your own progress.
- **Celebrate your wins:** Got out of bed? That's an Olympic-level achievement. Finally answered that email? Congrats, Nobel Prize vibes right there.***
- **Be kind to yourself:** Mistakes happen. Learn, move on, and be gentle with yourself in the process.
- **Listen to your body:** If your body is whispering for a nap, don't wait until it's screaming to take a break.
- **Disconnect from tech:** Take regular breaks from screens to recharge and improve your mental clarity.
- **Seek professional help:** If burnout feels too overwhelming, talking to a therapist or counselor can make all the difference.

---

* Unless the person you're comparing yourself to is yesterday's version of you. In that case, go ahead and flex.

** I see you: social media.

*** . . . For taming your inbox.

When we voluntarily embrace positive stress, we build our resilience and recharge our batteries, preparing ourselves to handle the unavoidable distress in life. By learning how to manage stress, we can move from a place of anxiety and struggle to one of growth, fulfillment, and joy. **Instead of constantly fighting stress, we can learn to dance with it,** using its energy to create a life that's truly unforgettable.

INSTEAD OF CONSTANTLY FIGHTING STRESS, WE CAN LEARN TO DANCE WITH IT, USING ITS ENERGY TO CREATE A LIFE THAT'S TRULY UNFORGETTABLE.

FEEL FREE TO USE THIS PAGE TO DOODLE

PART 8:

OWNING OUR POWER

46.

THOUGHTS

GO ~~SHAWTY~~ ANXIETY, IT'S YOUR BIRTHDAY

I sat in my car one morning on my way to meet friends outside the city, and I freaked out because something was missing; someone had stolen my steering wheel! Keys in hand, panicking, a second later, I realized I was sitting in the passenger seat. This has happened more than once in the past few years.

By the time this book comes out, I'll be 43 going on 44. I know my birthday gives me anxiety because it took 15 minutes to get the nerve to share my age with you. I flirted with being vague. I could have said I'm in my 40s, or, even more cryptic, I'm settling deep into another decade.*

Why does my birthday give me anxiety? It's a reminder that I'm getting older, and reminders are triggers. I'm at the age where working out isn't simply to look and feel nice. It's necessary maintenance so I don't fall apart. As I get older, I also feel more and more irrelevant to the world, as if I'm slowly being nudged out by the newer generation and put out to pasture. From a relationship standpoint, I feel like the older I get, the less desirable I am and the less likely it is that I'll find a great partner.

All these thoughts make my survival brain feel there's danger and set off my anxious alarms.

There's plenty to be anxious about when it comes to our birthdays. As that "magical" day approaches, the anxiety starts to grow, making it less of a celebration and more of something to completely dread.

* Maybe some of you'd have believed it was my 30s, or even 20s—a guy can hope.

Birthdays can trigger **existential anxiety**, where we start questioning everything—our age, our life choices, and why we haven't mastered the adult skill of folding a fitted sheet. Facing our limitations and the passage of time can be really stressful.

Birthdays naturally make us reflect on our lives—achievements, relationships, and goals. This introspection can easily turn into self-criticism, where we focus more on what's missing than on our accomplishments. Our survival brain makes us focus on what's out of place, leading to feelings of loneliness and unmet expectations instead of celebration. Social media only makes this worse by showing us the highlight reels of others' celebrations, making our own lives seem lacking in comparison.

Our childhood experiences also shape how we feel about birthdays. If you had emotionally unavailable caregivers, birthdays might have felt more like obligations than celebrations. This sends the message that "your existence isn't something to celebrate," feeding a sense of unworthiness into adulthood. We continue to think we're unworthy to protect ourselves from others making us feel this way.

> *Turning another year older doesn't feel like progress when you don't believe you're worthy of celebrating.*
>
> — SARAH NOFFKE

Even if we logically know we deserve to celebrate another year of life, there's always that little voice saying, "Yeah, but what about those goals you haven't hit yet, like becoming a trillionaire or finally learning to parallel park?" That inner conflict creates mixed emotions: anxiety, sadness, maybe even anger. Planning a party starts to feel like setting yourself up for judgment, and suddenly, the whole idea becomes overwhelming.

Before you flush your birthday cake down the toilet, there are things to consider.

Being aware of our birthday anxiety helps us handle it better. Existential thoughts make our survival brain hit the panic button, even when there's no real danger. Instead of treating these thoughts like the enemy, we can use them to dig deeper and figure out what's really going on. These feelings usually stem from past experiences, not our current reality.

In *The Gifts of Imperfection*, Brené Brown writes, "Owning our story and loving ourselves through that process is the bravest thing that we'll ever do." Embracing our birthday as a celebration of our journey, with all its ups and downs, is a powerful act of self-love.

I've reclaimed my birthday by creating my own meaningful traditions.* I'm not into big parties or elaborate plans. Instead, I design a day that fits my everyday life. I get up early, work out, enjoy some great art, eat good food, stay productive, and have fun. My birthday is a reset—a new chapter where I set the tone for a life I actually enjoy living.

Your version of this might look completely different, and that's okay. The goal is to **celebrate in a way that feels authentic and nurturing to you.** For some, that'll be a peaceful meditation retreat. For others, it'll be 12 shots of tequila, a regrettable tattoo, and a full day of denying any crimes took place.** Either way, it's about honoring yourself in a way that feels right for *you*.

I'm writing this chapter on February 14,*** and my birthday is July 12th.**** I have five months, and I'm already creating an insane to-do list of things I need to get done so I don't feel like a piece of garbage on the day of.

What we, including myself, need to remember is that our birthdays aren't just reminders that we're getting older, uglier, and dumber. They're also chances to practice self-love, self-compassion, connection to others, and acceptance of things out of our control. Letting go helps us gain more and reduces anxiety over things we can't change.

Every day is a gift, and as we get older, fewer people are still on this ride with us. We don't have to wait for a full rotation around the sun to celebrate—waking up this morning is enough for a mini-celebration. This is life—a temporary vacation from not existing—and we deserve to make the most of it in every way that excites us.

So what if I sit on the wrong side of the car every now and then? If it keeps happening, I'll just move to England and claim I've been practicing all along.

---

* Like pretending I don't have gray hairs or reminding myself that naps are the real gift.

** Yes, it's one of my goals to have my book presented as evidence at your criminal trial.

*** I probably should have written a Valentine's Anxiety chapter today.

**** Save that in your phone and send me gifts.

IT'S HARD TO FEEL GOOD ABOUT YOUR BIRTHDAY IF YOU DON'T FEEL GOOD ABOUT YOURSELF.

HUMBLE THE POET

47.

HABITS

WE'LL NEVER FEEL READY

It's 2:31 A.M., and I need to book a flight for my friends Matthew & Audrey's wedding in Italy. I've known I needed to book this flight for months. I RSVP'd and everything, but the moment I opened their website with all the travel and accommodations information, I got overwhelmed and switched tabs to YouTube to watch subliminal diss songs between my favorite rappers.*

Now, just weeks away, prices are rising, and I still haven't bought my ticket. My mind starts conjuring excuses for bailing—sick puppy, vague "personal issues," or just bluntly saying, "I can't make it anymore." I start questioning if I even wanted to go to this wedding in the first place. Who was that version of me that agreed? The rabbit hole deepens, and now I'm questioning the whole institution of marriage, monogamy, and whether my attendance at this wedding means I'm silently endorsing outdated social constructs.

When Matthew invited me, he generously said, "No pressure at all. It's a long trip, and we don't expect anyone to come." Despite that perfect excuse, I still said yes.

So here I am at 2:47 A.M., bleary-eyed after looking at routes, calculating layovers, and wondering who's going to watch my puppy. I'm about to purchase my ticket, realizing whatever I save on the flight will probably disappear on a taxi, an overpriced airport coffee, or a "next round's on me" situation.

I hit Purchase, and the site starts processing . . . then redirects me to a page saying fares have gone up. It's 3:02 A.M. now. Maybe it's a scam, or maybe I really snoozed. Either way, I go ahead with the higher fare. The ticket is booked, and I'm too exhausted to even think about hotels.

* Patriotism requires me to say my hometown guy won.

I know the saying, **"ANY decision is better than NO decision,"** but I still procrastinate like it's a full-time job. I put off paying bills, sending emails, replying to texts, ending relationships—basically anything that feels uncomfortable. Instead, I distract myself with whatever feels easier in the moment. Then, when the pressure hits, I scramble to get it all done, stressing myself out and wondering why I always wait until the last minute.

I procrastinate because I tell myself I'm not ready. I think I need more information to make the *right* decision, but that just leaves me stuck in analysis paralysis. Anxiety tricks me into thinking things are more complicated than they are. Like, "I can't go for a run today; I haven't figured out the perfect playlist." Or, "I can't join the gym yet; I need to research every gym in my area first." Or, "I can't ask that cutie for their number; I need to first come up with 7,000 reasons why they'll say no."

And so the cycle continues.

But, Humble, aren't avoidance and procrastination the same thing?

No, my handsome friends, they are not. Picture this: There's a spider in your room. Avoidance is straight-up dodging the spider forever, like moving to the couch and hoping the spider eventually starts paying rent. Procrastination, on the other hand, is delaying dealing with the spider because you need to first figure out its zodiac sign, learn its hopes and dreams, social security number, and then research the most humane way to convince it to either leave or sign a lease.

Procrastination is something we all face, and it's not always bad. The problem is that the anxiety around a challenge can feel bigger than the challenge itself. So, instead of diving in, we distract ourselves for quick relief. It makes us feel like we're getting things done, but we're really just avoiding what matters. **Procrastination tricks us into feeling in control, but it actually leads to even more anxiety.** Our survival brain craves control when it feels threatened, and avoiding the task feels like control—but it's just stalling. The anxiety may ease for a moment, but the task is still there, waiting.

The goal is to find strategies that help us break the cycle of procrastination and actually get stuff done. To beat procrastination, we need to close the gap between thinking and doing. The longer we stay stuck in thinking, the harder it gets to start. Taking action, even a small step, helps us move past hesitation and eases anxiety.

Our nervous system acts like the wiring that connects our brain and body, shaping our thoughts, actions, and emotions. Within that system, there's something called **the interest-based nervous system** (IBNS). It's kind of like a bouncer at a club, deciding what info gets in and what gets ignored.

Many of us operate with an IBNS, and we're like explorers, constantly chasing new, exciting things to learn and do. While this curiosity is great, it also makes it harder to focus on tasks that don't seem as interesting. If you're trying to study, fold laundry, or pick up a new skill, your IBNS might be screaming, "This is boring, let's find something more fun, like scrolling through Instagram or diving into random Wikipedia rabbit holes."

This is because our brains run on a reward system. When we do something easy and fun, we get a hit of dopamine, that feel-good chemical that keeps us motivated. Procrastination is our brain saying, "Let's chase that quick dopamine fix instead of doing this hard task." While it feels good in the moment, it's temporary. Ironically, the longer we delay gratification, the stronger the dopamine response, making the experience even more rewarding. In the long run, procrastination cranks up our anxiety, leaving us stressed and overwhelmed, which only makes it harder to get things done. It's a cycle, and the trick is finding ways to break out of it.

By avoiding hard tasks and opting for immediate gratification, our brain thinks it's protecting us, but it's actually causing more harm in the long term. My survival brain's like, "Hey, let's scroll on our phones instead of answering that urgent email—it's self-care, right?" It's like that one friend who says, "You know what'll really help you focus before your final? Binge-watching an entire season of *The Office*. Trust me, it'll totally chill you out."

The common excuse our brain will make is "we're not ready" as a way to protect us. But the truth is, we're never ready.

*Procrastinating doesn't mean we're lazy; it means we're avoiding the tough emotions that come with doing something challenging.** Here are some simple tips to tackle procrastination:

- **Break down big tasks:** If running feels overwhelming, just focus on putting on your shoes. If that's too much, start smaller—just grab your shoes and see what happens.

* Yep, sometimes that "big, scary tough emotion" is just . . . boredom. Riveting, right?

- **Make the task interesting:** When I was writing this book, I'd challenge myself to spend just one hour at the keyboard, no distractions. Whether I wrote 10 words or 10,000, if I got through the hour, I'd call it a win.
- **Reward yourself:** Every bit of progress releases dopamine. Remember, Rome wasn't built in a day—tiny steps lead to big wins. Celebrate even the smallest victories.
- **Create a focus-friendly environment:** Don't rely on discipline. Turn off your phone and hide it in another room or your car. Make it hard to get distracted and easy to focus.
- **Talk to someone:** Share your procrastination struggles with someone you trust. It's a sign of anxiety, and talking about it can help you work through it.
- **Take breaks:** Know when you need rest and when you're avoiding work. If you're fresher in the morning, plan to tackle your hardest tasks then. Rest boosts productivity and helps manage stress.

By using these tips, you can slowly reduce procrastination and feel more in control of your day and your emotions.

When we focus on the anxiety and tough emotions around the things we're putting off, we'll be better equipped to get those things done.

Let's also remember that we need to take the actions to feel how we want, NOT wait to feel how we want to take the actions we need.

Update: I made it to Matthew & Audrey's wedding, and wow, what a journey. Honestly, I probably spent more time traveling than I did in Italy. The wedding was beautiful, the reception was a blast, and even though most of the friends I expected to see didn't show up, I made some awesome new friends—and ended up in way more group chats than I needed.

After the wedding, I headed to Barcelona for a week with an old friend and his family. Now living in Spain is officially on my list. Even though I procrastinated like crazy, the trip turned out to be filled with magical experiences that changed the way I see, love, and appreciate the world.

PROCRASTINATING DOESN'T MEAN WE'RE LAZY; IT MEANS WE'RE AVOIDING THE TOUGH EMOTIONS THAT COME WITH DOING SOMETHING CHALLENGING.

48. YOUR PARENTS' ANXIETY IS NOT YOUR RESPONSIBILITY

Have you ever felt like you've become more of a parent to your parents than they are to you? Maybe you're the one making sure the bills are paid, keeping the peace, and handling the family drama like an unofficial, unqualified, and unpaid therapist. As the youngest in my house, most of this weight was carried by my sisters. Seeing this pattern in other Punjabi households, it seemed like a natural part of our culture. But it's not just about doing more chores or helping our parents open a PDF—it's about carrying a weight that's too heavy for our age.

If you started taking on this role as an adult, you might cope better, but if you've been Family CEO since you still had baby teeth and velcro shoes, you're not alone. This is what it means to be a **parentified child**. It's like wearing shoes that are too big, trying to guide your family while struggling not to faceplant.

A parentified child is someone who has been forced to grow up too fast, taking on responsibilities and emotional roles that usually belong to a parent. For some of you, it may have been doing the cooking and taking care of your siblings because your parents couldn't. For others, it was being the translator and therapist to a parent struggling to navigate the world.

When children take on adult roles too early, it affects their development and mental health. They start worrying about future problems and stay on high alert more than they should. Many of us didn't choose to become the parentified child; it happened because of situations beyond our control. Looking back, it's important to understand how these experiences shaped our anxiety patterns, not just to blame our parents for why we feel messed up.

Anxiety, like eye color, balding, and snoring,* can be passed down through generations. Unprocessed emotions, unhealed anxieties, and unhealthy coping mechanisms can be inherited, passed from our parents to us through unspoken expectations and behaviors.** We often imitate our parents' behaviors and emotional responses. Again, recognizing these patterns isn't about placing blame; it's about becoming aware, understanding them, and breaking the cycle in our own lives.

We're not obligated to repeat unhealthy patterns that cause anxiety in our life.

When it comes to your parents, you're not responsible for:

- **Their guilt:** You didn't cause their past hurts, and you can't erase them. Their guilt belongs to them, not you.
- **Their worry:** You cannot control their anxieties and taking them on only amplifies your own.
- **Their shame:** Their choices and actions are theirs to own; their burden is not yours to shoulder.
- **Their unavailability:** You deserve emotional support and connection. If your parents can't provide it, you have the right to find it elsewhere.

You're not responsible for your parents' emotional well-being, and that doesn't mean you don't love them or want to help them. **Being there for your parents doesn't require you to carry their guilt, worry, or shame.** We can acknowledge their struggles without taking them onto our own shoulders. We can support and love them, but their emotions are theirs to manage, not ours. That means establishing clear limits on our responsibility for their happiness and emotional well-being.

It's crucial to prioritize our own mental health and set boundaries, even if it's met with resistance or guilt. *Making ourselves a priority isn't selfish; it's necessary.* As

* Thanks, Dad.

** Like old hand-me-down sweaters that don't fit but we're stuck wearing anyway—except these don't come from your parents' closet, they come from their emotional baggage.

the saying goes, "You can't pour from an empty cup." If you're all used up emotionally, you can't help anyone, not even yourself. You deserve healthy relationships where everyone takes care of themselves and supports each other, not just one person doing all the emotional weightlifting.

Remember, boundaries aren't the enemy; they teach people how to treat you. Think of them like the velvet ropes at fancy museums—they keep others from getting too close and accidentally knocking over the masterpiece that is your sanity. **Boundaries protect us from getting sucked into someone else's emotional drama.**

In your family, boundaries might mean saying things like, "I love you, but I can't listen to your play-by-play of the office drama again—let's save it for after my mental health has clocked back in," or "My room is my stress-free zone; no negativity allowed." It's okay if setting boundaries feels weird or impossible* at first—it's like learning a new dance move. You have to practice to get good at it, and mistakes are expected.

The godfather of deep, psychological insights, Carl Jung, once said, "I am not what happened to me. I am what I choose to become." This is your shot to finally decide who you want to be—someone with their own life, not just the family's go-to problem solver, human calendar, and emotional referee.

Breaking free from family-driven anxiety requires self-awareness, compassion, and courage. It's about recognizing the patterns, setting healthy boundaries, and focusing on your own emotional well-being. Remember, you're not alone in this journey. There are resources, support systems, and therapists who can help you untangle anxiety and build a life filled with resilience, self-love, and freedom from inherited burdens.

They built a whole house on my back,
calling it "family responsibility,"
but forgot to leave a window for my own breath.

— UNKNOWN

* Looking at you, immigrant kids.

My sisters and I divide up the "parenting" duties for our parents. And by divide, I mean they handle most of it while I'm the "remote support" guy. Being the only one who's not local, I feel more like a spectator in the family chaos and sometimes guilty for not pulling my weight. Both my sisters have three kids,* bills, and lives of their own. It's amazing to see how much they show up for my parents, leaving me to gallivant the globe, fooling myself into believing I'm a responsible adult with only a low-maintenance puppy to care for. At this point, all I can do is hope one of these books blows up, so I can gift them a family cottage on the lake.**

* It's actually two kids each, but one of my nephews is a 6' 4", 285 lbs. NCAA football player, and my other sister just got an oversized puppy, so I round up out of respect for their grocery bills.

** So, for the love of my sisters and their large families, please spread the word about this book.

YOU DIDN'T CAUSE THEIR PAST HURTS, AND YOU CAN'T ERASE THEM. THEIR GUILT BELONGS TO THEM, NOT YOU.

HUMBLE THE POET

49.

REACTIONS

LET'S TALK ABOUT MY DEPRESSION

Whenever I've written about depression before, I've practically built a legal fortress of disclaimers around it, suggesting that if you're relying on my beard for mental health advice, you might as well consult a houseplant for tax advice. The goal was to never minimize people who experience depression on any level, and if I ended up saying something that I thought was encouraging and motivating but someone else took as triggering or insensitive, I felt covered.

This time is different because my goal isn't to talk about your depression and what to do with it. It's to talk about mine.

I was still in school when mental health wasn't as common a buzzword as it is today. Back in the day,* when someone mentioned "mental health," your brain instantly went to images of straightjackets and asylums. Day-to-day stress was just part of life back then, and if you said you were struggling with mental health, people either didn't believe you or they believed you too much—and then avoided you.

I was in my early 20s when I went to a walk-in clinic because I was exhausted all the time. It didn't feel normal. I was juggling school and a part-time job, but I was getting enough sleep, yet I just couldn't focus. This was before smartphones, so my biggest distraction was a CD player on the bus.

I grew up in a vegetarian household, and I figured I might be low on iron, so I went to the doctor hoping to get iron pills. The doctor was a young guy, maybe 35, and after running some tests, he said, "Your blood looks fine. I think you might be depressed."

* Back in the days is defined here as the 1990's.

I raised an eyebrow. "No way. I'm not sad. I don't have anything to be sad about."

He chuckled. "You don't have to be sad to be depressed. Low energy can be a sign too. It's not always about what's happening in your life; sometimes it's just genetics."

He prescribed me antidepressants, and that's how my journey with mental health began.

Does having a doctor diagnose me with depression and prescribe antidepressants make me an expert on the topic? Not really. But I'm not sharing this story to prove I'm an authority. I'm sharing it because stories like this need to be told. This was the start of my journey in understanding depression—mine and the depression that ran in my family.

Our survival brain can't always tell the difference between a physical threat and an emotional one. It's like it's running on ancient software, treating every awkward hug or stressful email like a full-blown emergency. So, when something feels off, our brain jumps into high alert, leading to two closely connected experiences: anxiety and depression.

Anxiety is when our fight-or-flight mode goes into overdrive. It's like our inner caveperson sees a wolf and immediately thinks, "What if behind that wolf is a ninja butterfly, ready to strike?" The brain spirals into worry and fear, even when everything's calm.

Depression, on the other hand, is like hitting hibernation mode. Our ancestors would conserve energy when facing scarcity, retreating to survive tough times. So when life feels hard for too long, our brain dims the lights and lowers motivation, almost like it's telling us to "give up for now, save energy." It's a survival tactic that works great when there's an actual tiger in front of you, but not so much when it's just a bad breakup or a tough day at work.

Again, our survival brains don't know the difference between the danger of a tiger and a bad breakup, So, when life gets tough, it'll respond as if we're under physical attack. It tells us to "shut down," making us feel tired, unmotivated, and just generally down. But since these events aren't actually life-threatening, this reaction isn't as helpful as it used to be.

It took a few more years before I was diagnosed with depressogenic thinking.

Thinking: How we interpret events and situations in our lives.

Depressogenic: Something that tends to cause depression.

When we're stuck in depressogenic thinking, our brains write the same sad story about everything, on repeat. This was a huge *a-ha* moment for me because I could finally see the pattern, not just in myself but also in my family.

For me, it could be as simple as: "She didn't return my text; she must hate me," or "My first idea was rejected. I'll never catch a break."

There are a few ways depressogenic thinking works:

- **Catastrophizing:** Every mistake turns into a massive disaster in our minds. A bad test feels like failing our entire future; a fight with a friend means they hate us forever. It's like taking the tiniest problem and blowing it up to epic proportions.
- **Overgeneralization:** One bad day becomes "proof" that everything sucks and always will. It's like getting one flat tire and thinking, "Well, cars are a disaster, society's doomed, and I'm officially switching to llamas for transportation." Our brain takes one negative experience and applies it to everything, ignoring the good stuff.
- **Personalization:** Feeling like everything's our fault, even when it's not. Like when a bird poops on your car, and you're convinced it's because you didn't recycle enough last week. Our brain blames us for everything negative, even if we had no control over it.
- **Negative filtering:** It's like wearing eclipse glasses that only block out the good things, magnifying the bad—like noticing the one person who didn't laugh at your joke in a room full of laughter.*

At this point, many of you, like me, might be having those *a-ha* moments, realizing you have depressogenic thinking or depression. The important thing to remember is that this doesn't mean you're broken or did something wrong. It just means you need to move forward with more awareness than before.

* Looking at you, social media comment sections.

We're talking about our brain's ability to manage mood, and just like people are born with quirks—like an asymmetrical nose, a third nipple,* or one leg slightly longer than the other—some of us have brains that don't always work ideally in certain situations. That's how I've come to understand my own depression and depressogenic thinking. **It's not about finding a "fix" or a "cure"; it's about making adjustments in life to reduce how much depression takes over.****

A technique that's been helping me is called *somatic tracking*, which is a fancy term for paying attention to what's happening in your body without judgment. It's basically mindfulness's slightly fancier cousin. When we're feeling anxious or depressed, we might notice sensations like a heavy chest or a knot in our stomach. Somatic tracking is about observing these sensations with curiosity instead of reacting with fear or frustration.

Why does this work? It's like telling your survival brain, "Hey, I see you trying to protect me, but we're actually safe." This helps update our brain's outdated software, reminding it that emotional stressors aren't life-threatening. Studies have shown that paying attention to body sensations without judgment helps break the brain's "danger" signals, easing symptoms of anxiety and creating a sense of calm.

Somatic tracking, like every strategy in this book, is a skill that needs regular practice. It's helped me a lot, but consistency is key to seeing lasting results.

Depression and anxiety are like two sides of the same coin. Depression pulls you back, telling you to shut down and conserve energy (downregulation), while anxiety gears you up, getting you ready to face danger (upregulation). It's like driving with one foot on the gas and the other on the brake, and wondering why your brain feels fried.

These two often show up together, leaving you feeling both wired and drained at the same time. You might be worrying about everything while also feeling too exhausted to get out of bed. That push-and-pull can be confusing and exhausting.

* Should I copyright #ThirdNippleBrain?

** Insert a funny joke about the adjustments we have to make in life when we have an odd number of nipples.

So, how do we find harmony?* For depression, think about doing things that give you a healthy kind of stress—the type that gets you moving and energized. It could be anything from a brisk walk to painting or working on a hobby.** The goal is to get those feel-good endorphins flowing and break out of the low-energy vibes.

For anxiety, it's about finding ways to calm down. You could set aside specific "worry times," break big tasks into smaller steps, or set clear, realistic goals. Doodling can be a great way to stay mindful and grounded. Organizing your thoughts in a journal and keeping tasks on a to-do list also gives your brain a break from being on constant high alert.

Everyday stress can trigger both anxiety and depression, so the little choices we make—like what we eat, how much sleep we get, and staying connected with people who make us feel good—help our brain manage emotions better. It's also important to remember that as awful as anxiety and depression feel, they're temporary storms. Focus on being kind to yourself, recognizing your stress signals, and aiming for progress, not perfection.

These are just tools, not magic cures. Everyone's journey is different, and working with a therapist or counselor can help you figure out what strategies work best for you.

Those antidepressants didn't last long for me. They turned down the volume on my feelings, but it was like being stuck on the world's saddest playlist, where no matter what I tried to listen to, it looped back to Adele's heartbreak album. I remember telling friends about my experience with them and not getting the most supportive reactions. That made me question whether my depression was real or if the doctor was just trying to get me out of the office quickly.***

Since then, I've grown a lot and learned to recognize that my brain is running on some outdated software, and I've worked hard to update it for the modern world. One of the biggest things I've noticed is how small my world gets when I isolate. Sometimes I don't even realize I'm isolating. It's not until I leave the house to walk

* I like the word *harmony* over *balance*.

** I hear beard braiding is all the rage.

*** The flip side of free health care up in Canada; that's a whole other conversation.

the pup that I remember how good it feels to be outside in the sun and have even a short conversation with someone.

Sometimes depression or negative thinking feels so normal that we don't notice it. But when we change up our environment—even just a little—we start to feel the difference. I like to think of these little adjustments as my own personal accessibility ramps and automatic doors, helping me get out of the dark cave depression can put me in.

If you're struggling with depression, remember you're not alone, and you're not broken. Society's approach to depression is like trying to fix a cracked iPhone screen with duct tape—technically, it's a solution, but it's not really doing the job. **The world doesn't always accommodate the challenges of depression, but that's a flaw in the world, not in you.** Keep going, make small changes, seek the help you need, and know that your life is worth living and fighting for.

The opposite of depression is not happiness, but vitality, the pulsing force of life that is present in every living thing.

— ANDREW SOLOMON

If I said anything that made you feel worse or triggered something, I apologize. My goal isn't to downplay anyone's experience with depression; it's to encourage more open conversations about it and promote seeking help from professionals. My experiences and the way I talk about them are unique to me, just like the strategies I use to get out of my own funks. I hope you find people who truly get how you're feeling so you don't feel like you're alone in this.

I'm not here to "depression-splain" to you, but I will disagree if you think there's no one out there who can understand or help. This is your life, and you deserve for it to feel as good as possible. That also means taking responsibility for making that happen. No one can take care of you better than you can, so be your own best friend. Take that first step in understanding your relationship with anxiety and depression, and get the support you need—anything is better than nothing.

YOU DON'T HAVE TO BE SAD TO BE DEPRESSED.

50.

REACTIONS

IT'S NOT YOUR FAULT

There's an ongoing joke online about people who get a puppy to help with their anxiety only to spread that anxiety to the dog—that isn't Boogie. My pup Boogie is a painfully adorable mini goldendoodle* who embodies the entitlement of a princess, the kindness of an angel, the demeanor of a drunk teddy bear and the unlimited energy of a toddler snorting sugar.

From the first week I got her, I practiced leaving her home alone, one hour at a time, until her separation anxiety subsided as she realized I'd eventually come home. She learned her space and how to invade mine. At the age of three, she's flown over a dozen flights with me and has joined me in moving around six homes in three cities and two countries.

She's been really easy to give to friends to babysit when I have long trips. She enjoys the staycations at other people's houses because they often come with fewer rules, more treats, and all the attention. For a long time, I thought I hit the puppy lottery with this anxiety-free happy-go-lucky furbaby that just wants to play and cuddle.

Until it was time for our second big move.

During our first move from Toronto to LA, she watched our home change as furniture disappeared and the boxes piled up and didn't seem to mind. Her crate disappeared, and she got to sleep in the bed with me.** The change was stressful for me: from my apartment to my parents' for a week, to the airport, to a friend's, and then eventually settling in our own place two months later.

* Instagram: Badbishboogie

** Yes—I, like most dog owners, said never in the bed, and now she's always in the bed, plus she has two other beds of her own.

She handled that move like a champ. So, 18 months later, when it was time to do it all again—this time from Los Angeles to New York—I thought it'd be a breeze. And it was, until it wasn't.

On our last night in the LA apartment, there was nothing left but a couch and a few boxes. While I packed, I kicked a tennis ball around for Boogie to chase. After taping up the last box, I turned around to see if she brought the ball back, but she didn't. She was sitting there looking up at me, ears pulled all the way back, eyes extra "puppy dog'd," beside a puddle of pee.

We went for a walk an hour before, and, at two years old, Boogie had never had an accident inside; something was wrong. I realized she was sensing my anxiety. The truth was, this move from LA to NYC was much more stressful for me than the last move. I had more stuff to take, less help from others, and a bunch of things, including a car, that I still needed to offload or sell.

I felt incredibly guilty for causing Boogie so much anxiety that she ended up peeing. The apartment was empty, and the floors were concrete—she didn't do any damage—but my anxiety about *her* anxiety made it feel catastrophic.

It was all my fault. Why couldn't I get my life together and stop moving so much? Why did I get a puppy if I knew I'd be trekking around, unable to give her stability and routine? Why was I moving? What if it didn't work out? NYC is the most expensive city in the multiverse. What if I go broke? Why can't I be normal like everyone else? What am I running from?

My anxiety started whispering, "You're failing at life," and soon it was basically running a whole infomercial about all the ways I was screwing up, complete with flashing red CALL NOW graphics. The truth was, it wasn't a big deal, and there was no reason to spiral. But my logical brain was on break. Instead my survival brain decided to cycle through all the ways it was all my fault and how much of a piece of trash I am; this was making me feel worse, and that was a sign of a deeper problem.

Many of us carry self-blame from our childhood experiences, especially if we grew up in homes where conflicts were avoided or ignored. This can cause a unique kind of harm. When anger and frustration are never addressed, it can feel like we're constantly walking on eggshells, always anxious about what might trigger the next outburst.

In unpredictable environments, our survival brain stays on high alert, scanning for threats and setting off anxiety alarms over imagined dangers. As kids it's easier to blame ourselves because the alternative—that we can't control everything, and that those who are supposed to protect us can sometimes make us feel unsafe—is too scary. We don't want to see our parents as imperfect since they're the ones in charge. So, we assume the bad things must be our fault. We're like little emotional Roombas, constantly sucking up everyone else's mess. While this self-blame might temporarily calm our anxiety by making us feel like we have some control, it only worsens our anxiety and self-doubt in the long run.

This is a learned behavior and a totally understandable way for a child to cope. When we're young, we don't realize our parents have their own shit going on, and their tension often has nothing to do with us. So, we think, "If I were better, things would be different." Over time, that belief in our own faults becomes deeply ingrained. What started as a way to cope with childhood chaos turns into an inner critic that follows us into adulthood.

The root of these anxious feelings is our fear of uncertainty and dread of disapproval. **Blaming ourselves helps us make sense of things,** but it also feeds anxiety, making us think everything that goes wrong is our fault. This belief not only heightens our anxiety but also makes it harder to be vulnerable, which prevents us from forming real connections with others.

Here's what you need to remember: YOU ARE NOT IN TROUBLE.

Bad things happen. Sometimes you're involved, but often you're not. None of this reflects your worth or abilities. You blame yourself because, as a tiny pea-brained child, you were trying to make sense of overwhelming situations in an environment you couldn't control.*

Let's revisit and rewrite these outdated stories we told ourselves now that our brains have grown from peas to peanuts.** **Going from self-blame to self-compassion is an important step.** It's time to stop playing emotional Jenga with our lives. Let's gently pull out those wonky blocks of self-blame and replace them with a big ol' foundation of "I'm doing my best here."

* I should sell this as a fridge magnet.

** We're smarter now, but not THAT smart; maybe some of you are at avocado level.

Mom and dad were arguing over the mortgage before you barged into the room without knocking—that's why you got yelled at.

The guy who cheated on you because he's insecure and uses attention from women as a Band-Aid to snooze his own anxious feelings—that's why he's chasing other girls behind your back. It's not your fault; it's his story, not yours.

Many of us adore those who ignore us and ignore those who adore us. Being extra nice to that girl who barely replies to you will just make you seem foreign and uncomfortable to her—which gives her anxious feelings. That's why she takes three days to return a text, even if she's always on her phone. She's not into you, and that's her story, not yours.

Moving is stressful—it's meant to be—and you did your best. A little puddle of pee from your beautiful darling isn't the end of the world. If anything, she's just marking her territory as a "high-anxiety zone." It's her way of saying she feels the same way you do. Her sensitivity is helping you recognize more of your own. You cleaned it up quickly and went back to playing fetch with her. You didn't get mad, you reassured her with a scratch behind the ears and a kiss on the nose, telling her everything was okay.

Now, extend that same reassurance to the scared child inside of you. If Boogie can move on from her "pee-saster" with a belly rub and a tennis ball, you can give your inner child the same kindness—minus the tennis ball.

Forgive yourself for not knowing
what you didn't know then.
Be gentle with yourself as you learn.

— LISA FELDMAN BARRETT

It's not your fault, you're not in trouble, and it's going to be okay. Have a treat.

FORGIVE YOURSELF
FOR NOT KNOWING
WHAT YOU
DIDN'T KNOW.

CONCLUSION: THE *REAL* CURE FOR ANXIETY

I got my first tattoo at 16, and every time I got a new one, someone would say, "You'll regret those when you're older." They weren't entirely wrong—but not for the reasons they thought.

I don't regret my tattoos; if anything, I regret not getting more. What someone should have told me is, "If you love tattoos, get as many as you can while you're young, because the older you get, the more they hurt. Fill up your canvas now."

I learned this the hard way last summer when I got a small, simple five-word tattoo for my birthday. It was right below my sternum and took only 10 minutes, but I needed three breaks because of the pain.

This was a far cry from the younger me who could sit for hours getting inked on my ribs. It turns out I'm a wimp now when it comes to needles. But this birthday tattoo in my 40s was my silver bullet for dealing with some of my deepest anxieties.

Five words, three lines:

At Any

Moment

You're Dust

My Ayahuasca brother Vlad said it in passing on one of our long walks, and it made my shoulders drop. It reminded me of something my old friend Davinder said a decade earlier: "Our problems are only real when we forget we're going to die."

These words—this reminder—are the real magic pill I've been hinting at throughout this book.

> *Nobody exists on purpose. Nobody belongs anywhere.*
> *Everybody's gonna die. Come watch TV.*
>
> — MORTY SMITH

Yes, it's morbid. Yes, thinking about death can feed anxiety. But if you really let it sink in, it's actually freeing. Remembering that we're going to die puts everything into perspective. It shows us that most of what we worry about is pretty small in the grand scheme of things.

We all have our beliefs about life and death. For me, life is a temporary vacation from not-existing, and I know my brain, wired for survival, wants me to forget that I won't exist in a few decades. That's why I paid someone to stab me with ink-filled needles—to remind me every time I step out of the shower and look in the mirror.*

Our daily stresses won't just disappear, but **remembering our time here is limited can lighten the load.** When we realize we won't be here forever, those little anxieties—like nailing a presentation or picking the perfect outfit—start to matter less. That shift creates space to take action and choose behaviors that help us manage our emotions better.

Imagine waking up every day knowing it could be your last. Life suddenly feels more intense, but also more joyful. This mindset pushes us to take risks, embrace spontaneity, and focus on what truly matters. We might laugh more, love harder, and stress less about the small stuff. Remembering that I'm going to die reminds me that the energy I get from anxiety can come from a much healthier source: joy.

* I'm still working on my Terry Crews pec pop.

Too often we push joy aside, saving it for some distant "someday" while we sink deeper into our anxious routines. That lack of joy makes us chase quick fixes to numb the anxiety. But what if we made joy a priority? We won't be here forever.

And joy doesn't have to be serious. Humor is a powerful tool. If we're all on this wild ride together, why not find joy in the absurdity of it all? Next time anxiety hits, laugh* at how ridiculous it is to stress over things that won't matter in the long run. It's like a cosmic joke, and we're all in on it.

When I started writing this book, I thought I needed to prove myself. I planned to dive into a gauntlet of anxiety—darkness retreats, financial stress tests, even stand-up comedy—to show I was "qualified" to write about this emotion. But I quickly realized I wasn't doing those things to help my own relationship with anxiety; I was doing them to silence the anxiety I had about not being good enough to write this book.

I'm not a neuroscientist or a psychologist. I'm just a guy with a soft beard who writes books because I hated how T-shirts shrank in the wash, making them shitty merch, and figured books were a better thing to sell at my music shows.

I didn't write this book to be an anxiety guru or pretend I've got it all figured out.** I, like you, deal with anxious feelings every day and would do anything to have a book like this to help me find some calm. I'm just trying to sort out my own mess, and this book is me doing that out loud.

Along the way, I stumbled onto something important—something that gave me a deeper purpose for writing this book, even without a degree hanging on the wall:*** Anxiety is speeding things up, and not in a good way.

The faster we move, the more fear takes over. The more scared we feel, the more we focus on ourselves. And when we're wrapped up in ourselves, there's less room for compassion or kindness. Love can't thrive in rush and stress.

---

* Laughing is a great strategy to manage emotions, try it, like now. I can't hear you!

** And if you've stuck with me this far, you know how little I actually have figured out.

*** Fun fact: I have two degrees and use neither of them.

Stress makes us slower, sicker, dumber, and more stubborn. It also makes it harder to recognize how it's affecting us—kind of like how a drunk person doesn't realize how drunk they are, a stressed person doesn't realize how stressed they are, and the damage it's causing.

The more anxious I got, the less I thought about anyone else. I was too stuck in my own head to notice the world around me. And when I did look up, the world only fed my anxiety more. I was too stressed to call my mom, too preoccupied to stay in touch with friends, and too anxious to ask for help. Instead I isolated myself, basically pouring gasoline on my anxiety.

That isolation? It's not just a "me" problem—it's an "us" problem.

When we're stuck in our anxious bubbles, we're not just hurting ourselves; we're pulling apart our communities. We get so caught up in our own struggles that we forget we're all in this together. And that's the real issue.

Unity is our superpower. When we come together, life's challenges don't seem so overwhelming. It's like we've got an invisible shield against the chaos. But we can't unite if we're all trapped in our anxiety-ridden worlds. We need to break out of this hyper-individualism that tricks us into thinking we're alone in our struggles—because we're not.

Remember that magic pill? It's not just about facing our mortality—it's about realizing that while we're here, we're all in this together. And that connection? That's a real cure.

Social isolation is the fuel anxiety feeds on, and it's a serious health issue. **Being disconnected from others is as harmful as high blood pressure or obesity.**

Dealing with anxiety means practicing the skills to manage our emotions. A world where people can manage their emotions is a safer world. It's a less addicted world. It's a more respectful world. It's a better world.

Share this book and what you've gained from it with the people you care about. Not just the ones who seem like they need it, but also the ones who may be suffering in silence. Reach out to that friend who's been off the grid. Smile at a stranger. Every bit of connection chips away at the isolation anxiety thrives on.

And for the love of all the strands in my beard, practice what you've learned in this book. **Managing our emotions is a skill, and skills only improve through action, so practice, practice, practice** . . . and then practice some more if you really want to feel better.

I don't care about being remembered or leaving a legacy. I just want the world to be better while I'm still here. And if you're reading this after I'm gone, know that, like 50 Cent, I died trying.

Thank you for sticking with me through this book. It means more than you know. You're not just a reader—we're connected. And I'll keep trying to be there for you, so you feel a little less alone. Let's make our deeper understanding of anxiety go viral—not for likes or shares, but for real change. A world with less anxiety and more connection? That's a world I want to live in. And I bet you do too.

Remember, we're all in this together. Now let's go make some noise.

As you finish this book and return to the world, remember that the solution to anxiety isn't about getting rid of fear or seeking perfection. It's about embracing our shared humanity, understanding life's brief nature, and choosing to live fully in the only thing we truly have: this moment. Let this awareness guide you, bring you joy, and set you free.

We may not have all the answers, but we can choose how we respond to life's uncertainties. So embrace the chaos, and remember: life's too short to let anxiety steal your joy.

Here's to taking risks, leaning in to uncomfortable feelings, and finding joy in the little things—because that's how we make more of life's moments count.

Please don't let this book stay on the shelf, please share it with someone who needs it.*

* Or better yet, buy them a copy—my puppy has expensive habits.

LIFE'S TOO SHORT TO LET ANXIETY STEAL YOUR JOY.

HUMBLE THE POET

RESOURCES

CHAPTER 1: WE'RE WIRED TO WORRY

Putnam, Robert D. Bowling Alone: *The Collapse and Revival of American Community.* New York: Simon & Schuster, 2000.

Appleyard, Donald. *Livable Streets*. Berkeley: University of California Press, 1981.

CHAPTER 5: THE OVERTHINKING CRACKHEAD HAMSTER IN OUR HEAD

Neff, Kristin. *Self-Compassion: The Proven Power of Being Kind to Yourself.* New York: HarperCollins, 2011.

Frankl, Viktor E. *Man's Search for Meaning*. Boston: Beacon Press, 1946.

CHAPTER 7: HOME IS WHERE THE ~~HEART IS~~ ANXIETY STARTS

Picardi, et al. "Attachment and Parenting in Adult Patients with Anxiety Disorders." *Clinical Practice and Epidemiology in Mental Health* 9 (2013): 157–163. https://www.ncbi.nlm.nih.gov/pmc/articles/PMC3804926/.

CHAPTER 8: CLASSROOMS & CUBICLES ARE FULL OF ANXIETY

Psych Central. "Hurry Sickness: Effects on Your Body and How to Manage It." Psych Central. Accessed November 18, 2024. https://psychcentral.com/anxiety/always-in-a-rush-maybe-its-time-urgency.

CHAPTER 9: ANXIOUS FRIENDS = ANXIOUS YOU

Holt-Lunstad, Julianne. "The Power and Prevalence of Loneliness." Harvard Health Blog, January 13, 2017. https://www.health.harvard.edu/blog/the-power-and-prevalence-of-loneliness-2017011310977.

CHAPTER 15: DON'T "SHOULD" ALL OVER YOURSELF

Hanson, Rick. "Anxiety and Fear." Accessed November 18, 2024. https://rickhanson.com/topics-for-personal-growth/anxiety-fear/.

CHAPTER 18: TURNING FOMO TO JOMO

Przybylski, et al. "Motivational, Emotional, and Behavioral Correlates of Fear of Missing Out." *Computers in Human Behavior* 29, no. 4 (2013): 1841–48. https://doi.org/10.1016/j.chb.2013.02.014.

CHAPTER 34: WE CAN'T ESCAPE WHAT WE DON'T FACE

Muhuri, Pradip K., Joseph C. Gfroerer, and M. Christine Davies. "Associations of Nonmedical Pain Reliever Use and Initiation of Heroin Use in the United States." Substance Abuse and Mental Health Services Administration, 2013. https://www.samhsa.gov/data/report/associations-nonmedical-pain-reliever-use-and-initiation-heroin-use-united-states.

CHAPTER 35: A SHATTERED HEART CAN BUILD A STRONGER YOU

Kross, et al. "Social Rejection Shares Somatosensory Representations with Physical Pain." *Proceedings of the National Academy of Sciences* 108, no. 15 (2011): 6270–75. https://doi.org/10.1073/pnas.1102693108.

Fisher, Helen E. *Why We Love: The Nature and Chemistry of Romantic Love*. New York: Henry Holt and Company, 2004.

ACKNOWLEDGMENTS

To the stranger who violently attacked and robbed my father so many years ago: I was only four years old when we snuck into Dad's room while he slept to see his injuries. I learned that day that black isn't black—it's more purple—and that the gash on his forehead looked more like oil mixed with water than a leaking bloody hole.

I learned that the protective shield he installed in the cab he drove—our family car—could be a fun toy to play with when we pretended it was a police car. But I also learned it was a massive source of anxiety every night he left for work.

I learned that even though I didn't understand anxiety, I could feel it. And that this anxiety could decide the entire direction of my life.

I hated that cab. I daydreamed about smashing it into pieces. Ironically, I spent so much time trying to be "successful" so he wouldn't have to drive that cab anymore, that I missed his retirement party because I was lost in this journey.

So, to the stranger who violently attacked and robbed my dad so many years ago, I want to acknowledge you. You gave me my first memory of anxiety and taught me about all the things that come with not paying attention to it.

I hope you're well. I hope you got what you needed that night. I only wish you had realized that he would have helped you if you had asked. I know this because I help people when they ask—not because I'm a good person, but because that's what I saw my parents do. I thought that's how everyone's parents were, and that helping was a normal thing to do.

To everyone reading this: Anxiety leaves marks on all of us in ways we may not fully understand. I hope you revisit your earliest memory of it, not to relive the pain but to learn what it taught you. Hold space for it. Let it trash the hotel room of your heart, and listen to what it has to say. Growth starts there, and maybe something in this book can help you take that step.

. . . And finally—caffeine. You are my morning prayer, my afternoon mantra, and my midnight regret. Without you, this book might not exist—or it might, but it would be much shorter, far less coherent, and written by someone who actually slept. You are my muse and my tormentor. You're toxic, a massive source of anxiety, but here we are. I can't quit you.

Anxiety: The brain's way of signaling us to pay attention, often triggered by real or imagined threats.

Survival Brain: The part of the brain (amygdala) that reacts quickly to danger to protect us.

Logical Brain: The part of the brain (prefrontal cortex) that helps us think clearly and solve problems.

Triggers: Things that remind us of the past, often linked to earlier threats, which can set off anxiety.

Triggered: Reliving a past experience.

Catastrophizing: Jumping to the worst-case scenario and seeing danger where there isn't any.

Regulated Nervous System: A calm and steady state where we feel in control of our emotions.

Resilience: The ability to bounce back from stress and challenges.

Mindfulness: Being present and aware without judging our thoughts or feelings.

Social Capital: The support and connection we build through our relationships.

C-PTSD (Complex PTSD): Emotional wounds from long-term harm, like neglect or criticism, where PTSD might come from a single event.

Coping Mechanisms: Habits we use to handle stress, which can either help or harm us.

Overthinking: The act of replaying a problem in our mind, believing we're solving it, but often losing focus instead.

Trauma: Deep emotional pain from hard experiences that shape how we respond to stress.

Novel Stressors: Modern challenges, like social media or multitasking, that our ancient brains aren't designed to handle.

Comfort Zone: A mental space where we feel safe and unchallenged, but staying there too long can hinder growth and resilience.

Self-Compassion: Treating ourselves with kindness and understanding, as we would a friend, especially during tough times.

Equanimity: Staying calm and balanced, even in stressful or challenging situations.

Sensations: The raw physical signals our body sends us, like a racing heart, tight chest, or butterflies in the stomach.

Feelings: The personal meanings we give to our sensations, shaped by our thoughts, beliefs, and current context.

Emotions: Signals from the brain, deeply tied to memory, serving as a record of what we've been through and shaping our reactions to situations.

MANAGING ANXIETY IS A SKILL. SKILLS NEED PRACTICE. TAKE ONE STEP AT A TIME—CHOOSE WHAT FEELS DOABLE:

Anxiety is your brain's alarm system responding to real or imagined threats. It's not your enemy—it's just trying (sometimes clumsily) to protect you.

TO BETTER UNDERSTAND ANXIETY, PRACTICE:

LOW EFFORT

- **Naming It:** Say, "I feel anxious" instead of "I'm anxious." This separates you from the feeling.
- **Noticing Your Body:** Look for signs like a tight jaw, clenched fists, or a racing heart.
- **Reminding Yourself:** "This will pass, and I've handled things like this before."
- **Feeling the Anxiety:** Allow yourself to notice it without avoiding, distracting, or medicating.

MEDIUM EFFORT

- **Asking Questions:** Reflect on whether the anxiety signals real danger.
- **Reframing It:** Tell yourself, "My brain thinks there's a threat, but I'm safe right now."
- **Getting Curious:** Observe patterns—does anxiety show up in certain situations?
- **Labeling the Mode:** Identify whether you're in Chill (social connection), Panic (fight-or-flight), or Shutdown (freeze) mode, and how it feels in your body.

HIGH EFFORT

- **Journaling Your Triggers:** Write about what causes anxiety and your responses.
- **Journaling Your Reactions:** Track when you're in Fight, Flight, Freeze, Fawn, or Safety mode.
- **Working with a Therapist:** Explore deeper causes and practice personalized techniques.

WHEN YOU FEEL ANXIOUS, TRY:

LOW EFFORT

- **Breathing:** Inhale for four counts, hold for four, exhale for four. Repeat three times.
- **Cooling Off:** Splash cold water on your face, use an ice pack, or hold an ice cube.
- **Grounding Yourself:** Name five things you see, four you touch, three you hear, two you smell, and one you taste.
- **Repeating a Mantra:** Use phrases like "I'm safe" or "This will pass."
- **Writing It Down:** Transfer your worries from your mind to paper.
- **Holding Something Comforting:** Grab a soft blanket, stress ball, or favorite object.

MEDIUM EFFORT

- **Stretching or Moving:** Roll your shoulders, shake your hands, or take a walk.
- **Visualizing Calm:** Picture a peaceful place and focus on how it makes you feel.
- **Practicing Progressive Relaxation:** Tighten and release each muscle group, from toes to head.
- **Talking to Someone:** Share your feelings with a trusted friend or therapist.
- **Doing a Simple Task:** Try folding laundry, washing dishes, or watering plants.

HIGH EFFORT

- **Exercising:** Run, dance, or do jumping jacks to release nervous energy.
- **Breaking It Down:** Focus on the next tiny step of a big task.
- **Planning Ahead:** Create a list or schedule for upcoming stressors.
- **Facing Triggers Gradually:** With support, practice exposure to rewire your responses.

TO SET YOURSELF UP FOR CALMER DAYS, PRACTICE:

LOW EFFORT

- **Sticking to a Routine:** Maintain regular sleep, meals, and downtime.
- **Limiting Screen Time:** Set boundaries on social media and news.
- **Hydrating:** Drink water throughout the day.
- **Spending Time Outside:** A few minutes of sunlight and fresh air can boost your mood.

MEDIUM EFFORT

- **Practicing Gratitude:** Recall a moment you're thankful for and immerse yourself in it.
- **Tidying Up:** Create a clean, calming space for relaxation.
- **Practicing Daily Movement:** Walk, stretch, or do yoga for 20–30 minutes.
- **Using Calming Tools:** Light a candle, sip tea, or listen to soothing music.
- **Doing Hobbies:** Engage in creative activities like drawing, cooking, or gardening.

HIGH EFFORT

- **Stepping out of Your Comfort Zone:** Try something new, even if it feels scary.
- **Meditating:** Start with one minute of sitting still and add a minute each day.
- **Setting Boundaries:** Learn to say "no" to things that drain your energy.
- **Working on Self-Compassion:** Talk to yourself as you would a friend.
- **Building Resilience:** Face challenges when you feel strong—it prepares you for tougher times.

FINAL THOUGHTS

You don't need to do everything at once. Start small by choosing one practice that feels doable today. Over time, these small steps add up, and managing anxiety becomes easier.

Remember: Practice makes progress. You've got this!

'The gateways to wisdom and knowledge are always open.'

Louise Hay